AF326585

VIDEO MAKING FOR BEGINNERS

DISCOVER THE PROVEN TECHNIQUES USED BY PROS TO CREATE HIGH-QUALITY PROFESSIONAL VIDEOS FOR LESS COST AND IN LESS TIME EVEN WITHOUT EXPERIENCE

TECHED PUBLISHERS

CONTENTS

Part III
CREATING YOUR STAGE

Part V

POST PRODUCTION

A Free Bonus To Our Readers

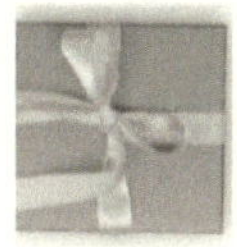
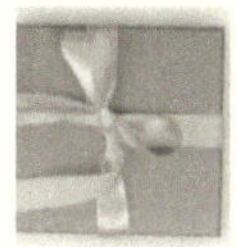

To get you started on using videos for social media, we have created:

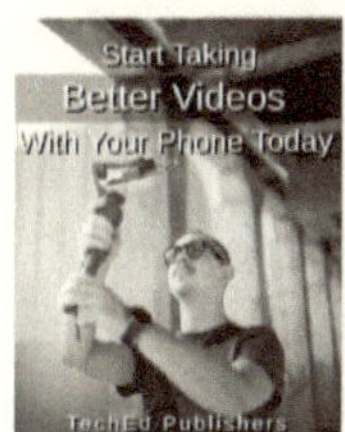
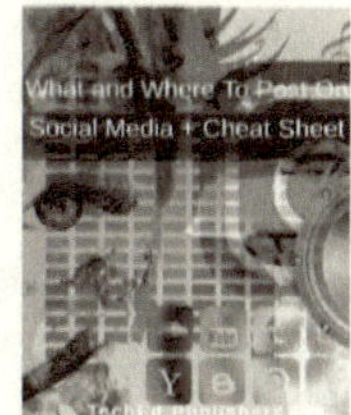
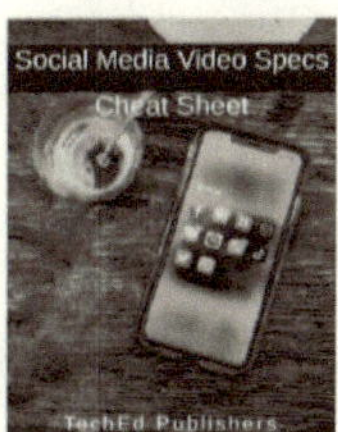
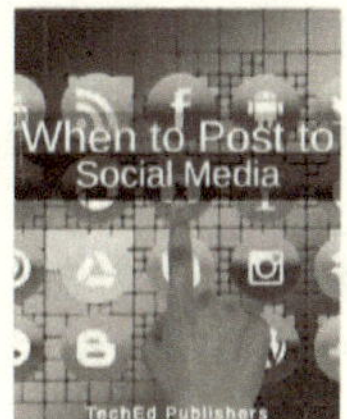

Free Bonus #1

Start Taking Better Videos with Your Phone Today

Free Bonus #2

What and Where to Post on Social Media + Cheat Sheet

Free Bonus #3

Social Media Video Specs Cheat Sheet

Free Bonus #4

When to Post to Social Media

With these free bonuses, you will

- Unlock the secrets to taking stunning videos with your phone today!

- Get a handy cheat sheet to guide you in creating the perfect content for each social media platform!

- Get a guide to create videos using the specifications of your chosen platform

- Determine the ideal times to post on various social media platforms and maximize the impact of your posts!

To get your free bonuses, please visit the link or scan the QR code below and let us know the email address to send it to.

pages.techedpublishers.com/bonus/vmfb

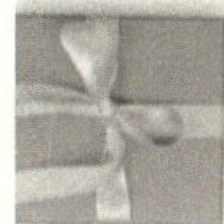
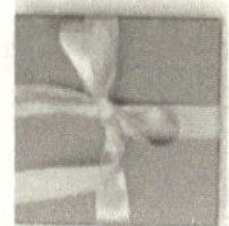

INTRODUCTION

"Video informs and entertains people and, good or bad, today most people prefer to watch a video than read a page of text."

–Lisa Lubin

Video is a powerful medium in today's technologically driven world. We can watch videos at any time of day or night, anywhere, and we have access to billions of videos from around the globe at the touch of a button. It's infiltrated every aspect of our lives, from entertainment to advertising to education. The truth is video is everywhere, but with more and more videos produced every day, it's becoming increasingly competitive.

Have you ever made a video, posted it on a hosting site, sat back, and waited for the views and likes to come rolling in, only for nothing to happen? Why do you think that is? Chances are, it's because, no matter how good you thought the video was, it probably wasn't good enough.

Producing a good video that people want to see starts well before you press the record button and only finishes long after you've stopped filming. There are individual steps in each part of the process. If you miss even one step, your video can quickly turn out a flop, and you've cottoned on to that concept. Now you want to know what you have to do to make better videos people will want to watch. Well, you've come to the right book.

In this book, we're going to walk you through the basics of making a good video, including:

Part 1: The equipment you need: video equipment comes in all shapes and sizes, so where do you begin figuring out what you really need and what it all does? In this section, we'll discuss the various devices you can record videos with and help you compare them. We even have a nifty feature comparison table to see the differences at a glance! Equipment doesn't stop with your recording device, though. We'll also delve into the various accessories you can add to your gear and how each helps improve your video quality.

Part 2: Planning and preparing: this is where many newbies make a big mistake. Just because you aren't making a big-budget Hollywood blockbuster doesn't mean you don't have to work out (and stick to) a budget or carefully plan how you will make your video. We cover how to divide your funds between the different phases of video production to prevent overspending in one area and running out of money for other vital steps in making a video. After the budget, planning your video is vitally important. We will take you through why setting achievable goals are crucial and how to set them. After that, you will learn how to write your video's story and script to effectively achieve those goals.

Part 3: Setting the scene: even if you are just filming an interview or webinar, your scene is just as essential as what your 'star' tells your audience. You need to know how to create a scene that supports the message you want to send and doesn't distract your audience. Background and foreground are powerful tools for sending subliminal messages. We will tell you how to use them to enhance your video. We'll also tell you how to scout locations to pick the right one and what you need to look for when selecting a location for filming. Then there's lighting. Video is all about light, so that's a pretty important aspect of your scene. You'll learn about lighting techniques, how to choose the right kind of light for your video, and how to use different lighting equipment.

Part 4: Filming techniques: a good video is like a good car ride. It's not all about the car but also the driver. You can take a ride in the best car on the market, but it won't be an enjoyable experience if you don't have a good driver. Learning fundamental filming techniques will instantly start improving your video-making skills. We'll cover the fundamentals necessary to improve the quality of your video during the filming stage.

Part 5: Post-production: Once you're done recording, you're only halfway done. Even the most amazingly filmed video can be ruined with lousy post-production. In this section, you'll discover how to make post-production better and techniques that will make your final video the best. Learning to take your video through the post-production phase takes time and practice, but if you start employing some of these basic techniques today, you'll immediately see a difference.

We'll discuss how choosing the right platform to showcase your work is as important as creating the video and we'll go through some of the popular video-hosting platforms and the pros and cons of each one to help you decide where to post your video.

Tips and tricks: When you're new to something, the learning curves involved can see you go through trial and error. Video-making is no different. Learning the ropes can be a tedious process (but very rewarding!). So, who wouldn't want to lay their hands on tips, tricks, and hacks that will make learning to create an excellent video easier? We've got you covered and will be giving you handy tidbits of knowledge to help you improve your video-making skills faster.

When you've worked your way through this book, you'll have the knowledge you need to start making videos that look more professional and leave the amateur label behind.

Whether it's a short film, product marketing video, how-to video, webinar series, video application to a college, or any other kind of video, we can help you make them better. All you need to do is keep reading to find out how to take your videos to the next level.

PART I

YOUR EQUIPMENT

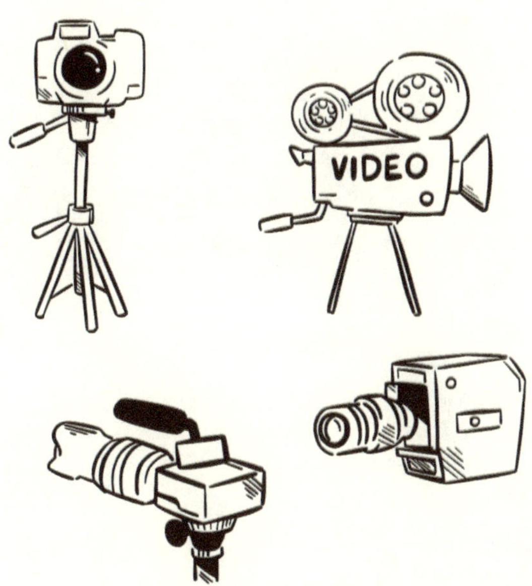

1

CAMERAS

Before you can begin your journey to making more professional videos, you need to know about the equipment. Do you need that budget-destroying professional-level video camera? We're going to take you through your options and the pros and cons of each. Not all of the equipment covered is strictly necessary; keep that in mind.

Tip: It can be tempting to rush out and buy equipment. Please don't do that. Please resist the temptation and wait until you've made it through the preparation and production parts of the book. Those parts of the video-making process will determine what equipment you need. Before you understand how to shoot your video, buying equipment could see you wasting money on the wrong gear.

The big question everybody wanting to improve their video-making asks is, "What type of camera do I need?"

"The best camera is the one that's with you."

– Chase Jarvis

No one has said wiser words in the photographic world. The same principle applies to video making. Don't have a proper video camera with you when something interesting happens? Whip out your mobile phone and capture it as best you can. The best camera you could have is the one that is actually with you when things go down.

Now, let's discuss video-making equipment.

TYPES OF CAMERAS

We're going to work through the options from the most basic and budget-friendly to the most high-tech and expensive option.

Mobile Phones

Mobile phone cameras for stills and video are continually advancing. It's pretty astounding how far technology has come. That said, we know we've just told you that your mobile phone will do the trick if you're in a pinch but is it the right choice to make a professional-looking video?

Camcorders

Depending on your budget and how much functionality you want from your camcorder, you have two design options. Entry-level camcorders are compact, portable, and fit snugly in the palm of your hand. Top-of-the-range camcorders come with a price tag relative to their functionality and look similar to a miniature professional video camera.

Prosumer Video Cameras

The prosumer video camera lies comfortably between consumer-grade camcorders and professional video cameras. They come with more controls and features and generally produce a better quality video. They also have a heftier price tag attached.

DSLR and Mirrorless Cameras

DSLR and mirrorless cameras range from hobbyist to entry-level professional to full-on professional. Built for snapping stills, some models have video capabilities.

Webcams and Action Cameras

Webcams have gotten a lot better over the years, and even the built-in camera on a laptop can record acceptable quality video. However, the quality they produce is nowhere near that of camcorders and DSLR cameras. You probably don't want to use a webcam for video unless you have no other option.

Action cameras are everywhere these days. They may be handy for on-the-go adventures but not for other types of video.

CAMERA CONSIDERATIONS

Now that you know which types of cameras are available, how do they stack up against one another, and what do you use to compare them? Below we've listed specific elements of a camera you should consider when deciding which camera is the best fit for the video you want to produce.

Physical Size

You want to think about the size and weight of your camera when moving from location to location. A larger camera doesn't travel as easily and conveniently, takes up space, and can become heavy after holding it up for a while.

Ergonomics

A product's ergonomics refers to aspects of its design that are intended to make it as easy as possible to use. Mobile phones are designed to be pocket-friendly, fit in the palm of your hand, and be used one-handed. DSLRs are designed to make it easy to take still images. Camcorders and prosumer video cameras have the sole purpose of recording video.

Controls and Features

Controls and features give you more creative control over your video. The number of controls and features varies according to the camera type and attached price tag. For instance, mobile phones only offer a fraction of what's available on an entry-level DSLR camera at a similar price point. In contrast, semi-pro and professional DSLR cameras cost more but offer more features. However, more features doesn't mean a camera will suit your needs better. Determine what features you actually need and choose a camera based on what you need and not how many features it has.

Ease of Use

Ease of use ties in with controls and features. The more you have, the trickier the camera is to use, and you'll end up spending more time learning how to use it. Simple cameras are easier to use even if they don't allow you to fine-tune your video in-camera during low-light recording.

Sensor Size

The size of your sensor affects the quality of your images and video. A smaller sensor doesn't have as many light receptors, and the image quality is poorer. Larger sensors allow you to capture more light and more detail for better quality.

Low-Light Capability

Shooting video in a studio with all the proper lighting is ideal, but things aren't always ideal. Your camera will need a larger sensor for low-light capability and should handle higher ISO settings. In general, full-frame cameras (larger sensors) have better low-light capabilities than cropped sensor cameras. However, it's important to understand that different cameras have different ISO thresholds, where they just don't like going above a certain ISO setting. You will only discover an individual camera's threshold by using it in different light situations but you can ask for advice from an experienced sales clerk when choosing a camera.

Dynamic Range

A smaller sensor is less likely to offer a decent dynamic range. Brighter or darker areas of your scene may lack detail, resulting in poorer video quality.

Interchangeable Lenses

For photographers, having different lenses means you have more options. Not all cameras offer you the opportunity to use different lenses, limiting your shooting capabilities. As many cameras offer zoom, it's not a make-or-break element for shooting video. Still, the extent of that zoom and the quality of the video at different focal lengths differ.

Multi-Functionality

How many things can you do with one camera? Some cameras can record videos, take stills, stitch images together to create a panorama, and more. Other cameras, like camcorders, are designed to do one job and one job only.

Battery Life

Battery life is a big one for shooting videos. Your camera's battery life dictates how much time you can spend shooting before you have to:

- Swap batteries if your camera has removable batteries

- Recharge the battery if you only have one removable battery or if your camera doesn't have removable batteries

Recording Time

How long are you going to be recording at any one time? If you're planning long shooting sessions, you're going to want a camera capable of continuous recording. Your battery life and the size of your memory card should be the only limitations.

Audio

An important consideration for choosing your camera for video is the audio capabilities. Audio is unimportant if you plan on muting your video and using backing track music. Otherwise, you're going to want good quality audio, so your audience can hear you properly.

Frame Rate

Also called frames per second (fps), frame rate refers to how many times your sensor is exposed to light per second. Believe it or not, cameras appear to capture continuous movement, as if the sensor is constantly exposed to light, but that's not what's happening in reality. Your camera is recording a bunch of still images, like an old-fashioned film reel, and those still images are being played back to appear as if they are continuous.

Some cameras offer more frame rate options than others. The frame rate you want depends on what kind of video you want to make. We'll cover different frame rates and which to choose for specific types of videos in Chapter 14.

Flip Screens

Some cameras have screens fixed in one position on the back. Those with flip screens, on the other hand, allow you to look directly at the camera and still see what the camera sees, you! When you're shooting solo, this is a significant advantage because you can adjust your position, lighting, and scene without having to run back and forth between the back of the camera and the front. Mobile phones may not have physical flip screens, but the selfie camera performs a similar job.

Accessories

Having accessories is the fun part of any camera. The more do-dads you have, the more creative you can be. How many accessories are available depends on the type of camera and what features and controls it has.

Rolling Shutter

You may think that a sensor is exposed to light all at once, so the entire sensor receives light in one exposure. This isn't always the case. Many consumer-grade still and video cameras have a rolling shutter where the sensor is exposed to light from top to bottom. Think of it as the sensor being scanned by the light.

A rolling shutter often leads to image distortions called rolling shutter artifacts. These distortions happen when you're videoing high-speed subjects. The sensor doesn't have enough time to be entirely scanned by the light each time to capture smooth movement. An example of a rolling shutter artifact is when a dead straight fast-moving object appears to have a curve that isn't actually there. As this is a common feature in many cameras, it doesn't mean you shouldn't use one that has a rolling shutter but if you can afford one, usually professional quality, then it's definitely an advantage.

VIDEO EQUIPMENT GLOSSARY

Aperture: The lens's aperture is controlled by moving mechanical parts and refers to the opening through which light enters the lens to reach the sensor. The size of the aperture affects the brightness of the image and the depth of field.

Depth of field: The depth of field relates to how much of the image is in focus. A shallower depth of field means less of the image around your focus point is in focus, while a wider depth of field means more is in focus. Depth of field is controlled by aperture, shutter speed, and ISO.

Dynamic range: How well your camera captures detail in bright and dark areas of your scene is referred to as the dynamic range. A higher dynamic range means more detail in those areas.

Focus: Focus refers to the clarity of the subject of your image.

Focus point: The focus point on your screen is the point you're choosing to be in sharpest focus.

ISO: The ISO function artificially boosts the light the sensor receives in low-light situations with the trade-off of increasing the grain or noise in an image.

Neutral density filters: These are optical filters that absorb all light wavelengths equally to reduce the harshness of outdoor light without affecting image color.

Noise: This refers to the amount of grain in an image or how grainy the image appears.

Sensor: This is the part of the camera that captures light to produce an image.

Shutter: Shutters can be mechanical or electronic. A mechanical shutter is a part of a camera, usually found in DSLRs, covering the sensor and is traditionally employed for still images. When the shutter opens, light hits the sensor, creating an image. An electronic shutter works by turning the sensor on and off. It does the same job as a mechanical shutter. Both DSLRs and camcorders record video using an electronic shutter to achieve faster frame rates due to not having mechanical parts.

Shutter speed: This is how much time the sensor is exposed to light measured in fractions of a second.

Video Format: Different cameras record video as different types of files. Not all video players will play all file types, but that's not the end of the world. Using a video editing software program, you can convert virtually any file type into another.

CAMERA COMPARISON TABLE

Putting the features and elements of each camera side-by-side in a table is the easiest way to see their differences and similarities at a glance. Please remember that this comparison table doesn't account for every variation of every model within a camera category. It is just a general overview. Some camera models will be an exception to a listed feature. Therefore, it's essential to look at each individual model you're considering to get the whole picture of your investment.

We aim to shoot quality video, so we will not list webcams and action cameras in this table. They have a specific time and place to be used, which isn't often incorporated in making a professional-looking video.

Feature	Mobile Phones	Consumer Camcorders	Prosumer Video Cameras	DSLR/Mirrorless Cameras
Physical size	Small + compact	Usually compact	Medium	Small – medium
Ergonomics for Video	Not ideal but workable	Ideal	Ideal	Not ideal but workable
Features and Controls	Limited	Moderate	Semi-pro	Semi-pro
Ease of use	Easy	Easy	Moderate	Moderate
Sensor size	Very small	Small	Medium	Medium – large
Lowlight capability	Poor	Moderate – good	Moderate – good	Moderate – good
Dynamic range	Not great	Good	Good	Good
Interchangeable lenses	No	No	No	Yes
Multi-functionality	Shoots stills + video	Video only	Video only	Shoots stills + video
Battery life	Variable	Variable	Variable	Variable
Recording time	Variable	Variable	Variable	Variable
Audio	Acceptable at close range	Good at close range	Good at close range	Acceptable at close range
Frame rate	Limited options	Various options	Various options	Various options
Flip screens ("selfie view")	Yes (backward-facing camera)	Yes	Yes	Some models

Important note: The table above represents average features across a spectrum of makes and models for each type of camera for video. Not all brands and models will have the same features, specs, capabilities, etc. It's vital to research the make and model of the type of camera you're considering to ensure you know what that specific camera's exact pros and cons are.

BOTTOM LINE

A good camera will help you create more professional-looking videos. If you don't have a video camera or DSLR/mirrorless camera, and you don't have the budget to go out and buy one, don't worry. The following parts and chapters of the book will help you use other techniques to create better videos without breaking the bank. Even your mobile phone can be used to help you employ the methods we're going to explore to get you started.

However, if you're going to shoot videos more seriously and regularly, buying or hiring a camera will definitely be to your advantage. Whether you've decided to purchase or lease, don't run out the door to your nearest store just yet. The following two parts will give you the knowledge to make the right equipment decisions. Let's get stuck in with the next chapter and look at additional equipment that will make your life so much easier and deliver better results when shooting a video.

2

VIDEO-MAKING ACCESSORIES

Video-making can be enhanced by using a variety of accessories. They not only allow you to produce more professional-looking videos, they also expand your capacity to really get creative. If you're serious about making videos that look good, here are some accessories you may want to consider investing in.

FIRST CHOICE ACCESSORIES

When we say "first choice accessories, we mean these should be your first priority to invest in when you're ready to get additional bits and bobs.

Tripods

Stability is critical when shooting a great-looking video. There's bound to be some movement whenever you hold a camera in your hand. Tripods are handy three-legged helpers that offer you two huge advantages. They offer you lots of stability and allow you to record video hands-free.

Tip: When fully extended, a tripod for video should reach a minimum of eye level to prevent you from having to stand hunched over while shooting.

Beanbags

Beanbags are a great option for shooting down low and getting the correct camera position on various surfaces.

Tip: If your budget is tight or you just need a quick beanbag on the go, you can even make your own. Sand or a material that doesn't absorb water is the best choice as filler, and the outer can be as simple as a Ziploc bag.

Lighting

Lights are your friend when it comes to shooting professional-looking videos. After all, video is simply recording light. Inadequate lighting results in a bad video.

There are four common types of lights you can use:

- **Halogen:** High-wattage, bright lighting, but they can get pretty hot after a while. They're ideal for filming.
- **Incandescent:** Low-wattage, light is less bright, and they'll tinge your scene yellow/orange.
- **Fluorescent:** low power usage and don't get hot. These lights provide soft, even light with bulbs in indoor and outdoor colors.

- **LED:** Efficient for various lighting techniques, affordable, bright, and low power usage. They're available in different color temperatures for color correction and shooting in multiple circumstances.

A word on halogen lights: It's not just the physical bulb that heats up and needs to be allowed to cool off completely before being packed up or moved. The bulbs also give off heat, like theater stage lights, which can make your subject feel hot and even start sweating. Filming time under halogen lights should be broken up into short periods to allow the subject to cool off and not overheat or start visibly sweating.

What key features should you consider when deciding on lights for making your videos?

- Adjustability between narrowing the beam to an intense point or spreading it out over a wider area.
- Durable stands that can adjust to different heights.
- Compactness and portability for easily carting them from one location to another.
- The power usage to keep costs down.
- The brightness, depending on what strength of light you need for your particular shoot.
- The color temperature depending on your needs.
- How hot the lights will make you or your subject and the temperature in your scene location.

Personal Computer or Laptop

Recording your video is one thing. Editing it is another. Video editing software programs are often 'heavy' and suck 'brainpower' from your computer and can slow it down while in use. It's essential to ensure you have a computer or laptop capable of supporting your video-making needs. These are the most crucial features to look for:

Storage space: 500GB hard drive minimum, but bigger is better. Consider a solid-state drive, or SSD, instead of a conventional mechanical hard drive for faster speeds.

Memory or RAM: Random-access memory is where your computer temporarily stores the information it is actively using at the time. It's where programs, like video editing software, store the data as you're using it so it can quickly be retrieved. More RAM equals a faster system. Opt for a minimum of 16GB.

Processing unit: The speed of your central processing unit, or CPU, contributes to how fast your system and software runs. Choose a multicore CPU with a minimum of 6 cores, but 8 to 12 is better. Look into a computer with a CPU running at 3.0 GHz or faster.

Graphics card: The graphics card will depend on the video editing software you choose. An NVIDIA or AMD card with a minimum of 2GB of memory is ideal, but more is better.

Operating system: Another contributing aspect to your system speed is the operating system or OS you're using.

Newer operating systems are designed to be faster, so lean toward the most recent version. You should also go with the 64-bit option if you're using Windows.

Screen size: The larger your screen, the better you can view your video while you're editing it. Good screen size is 19 to 21 inches, but 14 to 17 inches will also do the trick.

Screen resolution: Many video recorders, including mobile phones, offer the option to shoot in 4K, so you should be using a minimum of a 4K screen.

Editing Software

Once you have a computer with the appropriate specs for video editing, it's time to look at the software. There are loads of options, but they're not all created equal. Most video editors will use semi-pro software, such as Adobe Premiere Pro, Final Cut Pro, or Da Vinci Resolve. Here are the settings to look for in editing software:

Budget: The first thing that will decide what video editing software you choose is your budget. A rule of thumb is that cheaper software is usually more basic and limited.

User interface: When you first look at the software interface, it will probably look completely alien, even overwhelming. Compare user reviews on whether the interface is intuitive and user-friendly once you've learned to use it.

Input formats: Your video editing software should be able to accommodate a variety of video file formats. However, to ensure compatibility, you will have to know what file formats you will be using, which will depend on what you are recording with and the source files.

Editing tracks: Tracks are like layers. For instance, you may want to mute the original audio. You might go on to lay music over the muted video and then lay narration over it all so that you're seeing the video and hearing both the music and narration simultaneously. How many tracks do you really need?

- one for the main video
- two for video overlays (but one will do)
- two for still images
- one for titles
- one for subtitles
- one for music
- one for narration/voice-over

Good editing programs will offer you the option to build a video using more than enough tracks, but it's good to make sure you can use at least 8 or 9 channels.

Transitions: Transitions refer to how your video moves from one clip to another. Professional video makers generally avoid using transition effects. However, if you have a jarring difference between two clips, using a discrete transition doesn't hurt. Discrete means it doesn't twirl, whirl, flip, sparkle, etc., making it the video's star.

Common discrete transitions include

- Dissolve or cross-fade
- Fade to black

Filters and special effects: Don't be fooled by flashy and fancy special effects. Some simple effects and filters may help create a better looking video, but don't be tempted by the idea that more is better.

Audio: Audio is a prominent part of any video. Go with software that supports the latest version of Dolby and includes it in the purchase price. Compare user reviews on software audio capabilities to help make your decision.

File output: Different platforms and devices will favor different output formats. Check whether or not the software offers the ideal format for your chosen platform. Even better, to make your life simpler, look at whether the program tells you that the format is for YouTube, Facebook, Computer, TV, etc.

Memory Cards

Memory cards come in various physical sizes, capacities, transfer rates, and qualities. Transfer rate is how quickly the video is transferred from the sensor to the memory card. If you are shooting in 4K, you should be using memory cards with a minimum rate of 30Mbps, but you can't go wrong with a higher transfer rate. Factors that contribute to needing a higher transfer rate include whether you are shooting in RAW or at a higher resolution.

How long are you filming for, what format are you filming in, and what is the resolution of your video? Shooting in RAW, using a higher resolution, or shooting for longer periods requires a higher storage capacity.

SECOND CHOICE ACCESSORIES

These accessories are nice to have but aren't as crucial for improving your videos as the first choice accessories.

Gimbal

Gimbals stabilize your camera on three axes to keep your footage level and combat shake.

Tip: Some gimbals are designed to be used alone. Others are intended to be used both handheld or attached to your tripod. Decide what you're using it for to pick the right one.

Dummy Battery

A dummy battery can help you extend your recording time. It's not actually a battery. It's an adapter that fits into your camera's battery slot and allows you to plug it directly into mains power.

Spider Rig and Camera Cage

A spider rig is a foldable rig or frame that can take on a variety of shapes to accommodate different shooting requirements. You can use a spider rig in various situations, such as shooting from a low angle or stabilizing your camera for shooting at shoulder height.

A camera cage can be seen as a rig, grip, housing, bracket, or mount that does multiple jobs. It's designed to make a DSLR or mirrorless camera easier to use as a video camera. A camera cage:

- Helps protect your camera
- Makes handholding easier
- Offers you multiple points for mountain video-making accessories

The only downside of a camera cage is that it's not one-size-fits-all. You'll have to shop around for one that fits your camera, and if you have multiple cameras, that may mean having to invest in more than one cage.

Lens Filters

Many camcorders and prosumer video cameras come with a built-in neutral density filter. DSLR camera lenses don't. Neutral density filters make shooting outdoors easier, and the results are less blown out in bright light. Here are some other common types of lens filter and their uses:

- Polarizing filters help you get great definition outdoors by eliminating reflections, combatting glare, and adding extra saturation to colors.

- Color correction filters correct inconsistent color lighting for color that's more accurate.
- UV filters don't make much difference when using a digital camera, but they offer lens protection from scratches and other wear and tear. It's more cost-effective to replace a simple filter than a lens.

Capture Cards

A capture card is a device that allows you to live stream by linking your camera to a computer. It's not strictly necessary, as you can use a webcam. However, it's helpful if you're making more professional-looking live stream videos.

BUY OR HIRE?

When making a video, you can go out and buy your own equipment or hire it. How do you know when you should bite the proverbial bullet and shell out cash to purchase the gear and when to rent instead? Ask yourself these essential questions:

- What is your budget right now?
- What is the size of the project? How long will it take to film and edit, and what is the financial return likely to be?
- How many videos are you creating annually?

First and foremost, your budget will dictate whether you hire or buy. If you don't have the bank balance to purchase but can afford to rent for the duration of your shoot, that's what you're going to have to do until you've saved up the capital to invest in your own gear.

If you are working on a lengthy project, buying equipment may be more cost-effective. However, if you're working on a short video that you can film and finish up in a few days, renting the equipment is probably more economical.

Then consider how many videos you will be making in a year. Renting equipment may only be economical when making a handful of videos per year. If, however, you're putting out a video each week, the cost of hiring the equipment can quickly add up to the same amount as purchasing your own.

Spotting Fake Equipment

The world is full of people trying to make a quick buck by pulling the wool over your eyes. If you're going to purchase your own video-making equipment, you need to know how to spot counterfeit gear and avoid being duped into wasting money on a dud. Here are some top tips for avoiding fake equipment:

- Buy your gear from a reputable seller known for providing quality equipment.
- Make sure there's a warranty. All quality brands offer a warranty on their products. Fakes don't.
- Make sure it has a serial number. This doesn't necessarily hold true for accessories. However, a

camera, lenses, microphones, and other electronic and technical equipment should have a serial number somewhere on them.

- Look for official stickers containing holograms. Many brands include these on their boxes, and they're not easy to fake.
- Check the spelling. The real deal won't have misspellings on the box or on the equipment itself.
- Is the printing clear? Fake gear may be indicated by illegible printing on the box or paperwork.
- What is the price in comparison to the same thing from other distributors? If it's a bargain that seems too good to be true, it probably is.

Even if the box looks legitimate and like it contains the real deal, that may not be the case. Containers are easy to replicate, so don't allow appearances to hoodwink you into parting with your money for counterfeit equipment.

BOTTOM LINE

You now know more about the types of cameras and accessories that are available. We've also walked you through deciding whether to bite the bullet and purchase or hire what you need. You even now know how to spot fake equipment.

This first part of the book is crucial to understanding the techniques we'll cover later. While you read the following two parts of the book, keep in mind everything you've learned about equipment. This will help you better understand the camera and accessories you may need. In the next part, we delve into all the aspects of planning and preparing to shoot a video. Think again if you thought you could just take an idea and run with it. Lack of planning is one of the biggest mistakes you can make. It may be even more detrimental to the quality and efficacy of your video than not having pro-grade equipment.

PART II

PREPARING TO SHOOT YOUR VIDEO

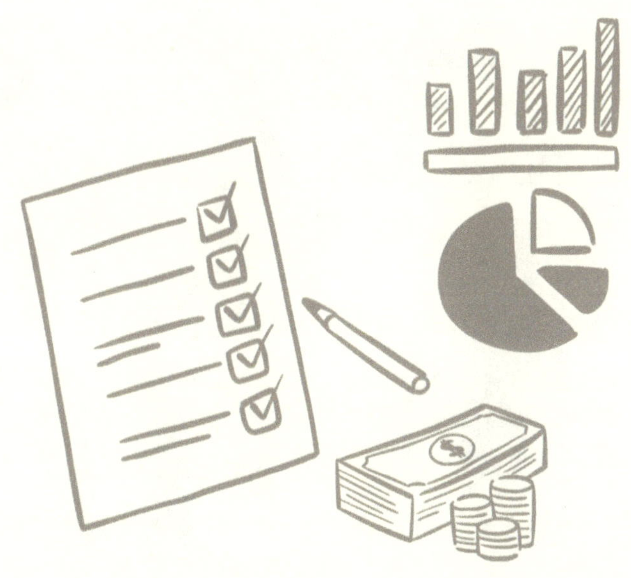

3

SHOULD IT BE A VIDEO?

Before you start planning your video, ask yourself something fundamental. Should this be a video, and why should it be a video?

EVIDENCE OF VIDEO SUCCESS

"If a photo is worth a thousand words, what's a video worth?"

–Unknown

There are a lot of compelling statistics to promote the power of using video for a variety of purposes, from marketing to education to entertainment. Let's look at some of the statistics published by techjury.com on the 4th of January 2022:

- 50% of online users in the United States watch videos daily.
- 81% of businesses today use video as a means of marketing due to its efficacy.
- The average person in the US watches around 323 minutes of video content on their mobile phones per week (not including other devices like laptops).
- YouTube is currently the most popular video platform online, with more than 2 billion users and YouTubers collectively uploading around 500 hours of footage every minute.
- A whopping 49% growth rate increase is seen in businesses that use video as a marketing tool compared to their non-video counterparts.
- An incredible 93% of businesses report increasing their customer base by combining video marketing with social media platforms.
- Despite being a seemingly text-based platform, 82% of today's Twitter users use the platform mainly to watch videos.
- Every day Facebook videos are viewed by more than 500 million users.
- After watching a video advertisement, 75% of Instagram users further look into the brand/products/services. Of those users who investigate further, 72% actually make a purchase.
- The total of all the TV footage broadcast by three large American TV networks over the last 30 years is

equivalent to what gets uploaded online in 30 days today.

WHAT SHOULDN'T BE A VIDEO?

With all those positive statistics pointing to the power of using video, why wouldn't you want to turn your content into video? Some content isn't particularly suited to videos, like facts and figures. Facts and figures are often dull, and you lose interest pretty quickly. You're likely to annoy and alienate your target audience if your whole video is centered on that type of content.

Let's take a look at an example:

You own a used car sales business that offers a wide variety of makes and models in excellent condition at reasonable prices. You now want to make a video to promote your business and show your target audience what you offer them. The stereotypical concept of an older car ad may come to mind. You know the one we're talking about. It's the ad where a car salesman in a cheesy suit walks through his lot of used cars for sale. He's yammering about the various makes and models on offer and their affordable prices. Even someone interested in buying a second-hand vehicle will be bored almost to death after just 30 seconds of this.

However, if you turn the concept into a story, you are more likely to capture viewers' attention. Let's say your video starts off with a young boy admiring a model car on the shelf in his bedroom, the exact car he dreams of owning as an adult. You then transition to the boy as a teenager, working hard to earn and save money for his dream car. You quickly cut to a shot of this boy taking his savings to your lot. He picks out his dream car and pays for it before panning to an aerial shot of your lot, showing the variety of vehicles you have to offer.

Can you see how the second advertisement conveys emotion? It's something that gets viewers drawn in. They may even relate to it. The video also shows what you have to offer and their affordable prices. In that story that evokes emotion from viewers, you've told your audience who you are, what you offer, and that you are not just a stiff in a suit trying to sell your wares. Your video is focused on telling a story with facts and even figures. Yet, it's not an infinitely boring series of makes, models, and prices.

Tip: Sometimes, it's impossible to get away from mentioning facts and figures in a video. If you need to include them, make sure your video doesn't revolve purely around them. It needs to remain entertaining. You should also keep them to a minimum and focus on facts and figures that naturally fit your narrative. You can also try sneaking them into your video in such a way that they aren't dominating your content but are subtly there for viewers to see.

Let's consider the example above. You may want to include facts and figures like the number of vehicles and satisfied customers you've dealt with and how affordable your prices are. You'd want to do this without scrolling text across the screen or the car salesperson telling the audience. For instance, in that final panning shot, you could have a nice, big signboard on the side of your office stating how many cars you've sold, and you could have the prices in the windows of the vehicles. That way, viewers perceive that you're reliable, give good service, and have affordable prices without allowing any part of your video to become all about those facts and figures.

BOTTOM LINE

Some ideas are better conveyed through text, blogs, or other formats to have maximum impact. Then there are the ideas that benefit more from being made into a video. Videos are great, but you should consider their efficacy. What format will get your message across effectively? If video is the way to go, the next chapter involves setting up that all-important video-making budget. Your budget is vitally important because it dictates what you can and cannot do when creating your video.

4

THE VIDEO BUDGET

"A budget is telling your money where to go instead of wondering where it went."

–Dave Ramsey

Let's talk about your budget. It is the most crucial aspect of planning your video. When you decide to make a video, you will have a general idea of what it will be about. However, before you even start fine-tuning that idea into more detail, you need to know how much you have available to spend on the whole project. When you know what you have in the bank, you can make critical decisions from an informed perspective. This avoids splurging on unnecessary elements, skimping on the important stuff, and running out of funding part-way through the project.

Considerations for drawing up a video budget include:

- What are the things you absolutely have to shell out cash for, the unavoidable costs?
- What can you barter for or even get for free?
- Will it be more cost-effective to buy equipment or accessories you don't already own or hire them?

Budget breakdown: There are four main areas in a video budget, and we will now look at a general breakdown of how much of your funds should be dedicated to each area:

PRE-PRODUCTION:10%

Everything that happens before you press that record button falls into this area of making a video. Dependent on what kind of video you're making, this includes but is not limited to:

- Scouting locations
- Stationary for creating storyboards, scripts, etc.
- Airtime, data, and other communication costs
- Services such as scriptwriters, casting directors, couriers
- The cost of traveling to and from meetings with others involved

Pre-production comes down to every little cost of getting you from the initial idea for the video to the day you start filming.

PRODUCTION: 35%

The production stage of your video may take up the most significant chunk of your budget but that's not always the case depending on the post-production. This area accounts for every expense involved with filming your video and includes but is not limited to:

- Paying your cast and crew
- Transportation for cast, crew, and equipment to filming locations
- The hiring of locations or permits needed to shoot in some locations
- Catering and beverages
- Accommodation for multi-day filming in locations away from where cast or crew live
- Rental rates for equipment
- An unspecified amount of budget for unforeseen costs, such as renting additional gear you may not realize you need or getting gear fixed if it breaks mid-production

Important note: Even if you're shooting a video solo, you will still have to budget expenses like food and beverages. The cost of food on the go is often higher than reaching into your fridge at home. Don't overlook any costs, or you could run into a budget blunder at the end of the day.

POST-PRODUCTION: 35%

The portion of your budget you allocate to post-production comes down to the type of video and how involved you will be. When it comes to deciding on your post-production budget, there are two scenarios.

Scenario one: You're making a basic video and have the knowledge and experience to do all your own post-production work. You only really have to take expenses such as your time, possible music licensing, and maybe stock footage costs into account.

Scenario two: Your video is more complex, and you don't have the post-production knowledge and experience yourself. In this situation, post-production should be allocated an equal percentage of your budget as production. You can film fantastic footage, but if the video isn't put together correctly and the audio mix isn't right, none of that will matter. You're going to have to pay someone else to do it for you. More people will need to be involved in larger, more complex projects.

MARKETING AND DISTRIBUTION: 20%

Marketing and distributing your video is the last step to getting your project out into the world and seen by your audience. This is the part of drawing up a video-making budget that most people tend to neglect. They focus on making the video and don't stop to think about what will happen if they don't have the bucks to finance getting it out there.

Sure, simple marketing and distribution can be done for free, but chances are, your video will not be seen by a broader audience. So, even if you post it on a social media platform, you're still going to have to invest in marketing, such as running social media ads.

Other aspects of marketing you should consider include:

- Creating a professional-looking website for your video (especially if you plan on using the video as part of building a brand)
- Potentially hiring a publicist to help you with your marketing strategies
- Placing advertisements on social media, online publications, etc.
- Holding screenings at locations such as theatres, festivals, etc.

Tip: As with the other sections of your video-making budget, always keep an eye out for opportunities to bargain or barter for the services you need.

BOTTOM LINE

Your budget is critical and will help you in the next part of planning your video. You may come up with ideas that won't fit into your budget, and you'll come up with ideas that do.

Allowing your creativity to flourish means not focusing solely on your budget while you're planning your video. However, having a budget will help you determine which ideas you can and can't execute. The next chapter deals with setting goals for your video-making project. These goals aren't necessarily budget-related, but they set the stage for the creative process we explore in the chapters following goal-setting. So, let's get into setting those goals.

5

SET SMART VIDEO-MAKING GOALS

"Setting goals is the first step in turning the invisible into the visible."

–Tony Robbins

Before you can even pick your camera up, never mind hit that record button, you need to set goals and not just any goals. You need to set SMART goals.

SMART goals are:

- **S**pecific
- **M**easurable
- **A**chievable
- **R**elevant
- **T**ime-bound

Let's delve into how each of these terms applies to creating a plan for making your video.

SPECIFIC

Being specific about your video covers various aspects, so sit tight as we walk you through all the areas you need to be clear about to narrow your video ideas down.

Video Identity

Your video's identity relates to the aim the footage wants to achieve, or perhaps, you can think of it in terms of the genre. Genres aren't just for films. Every video has a genre or a label you can attach to it that sums up the type of video based on what it's meant to achieve.

For example, a movie in the horror genre is meant to give viewers the creeps and maybe even make them jump out of their seats. A marketing video is intended to give viewers a clear, positive overview of the brand, what the organization does, what the product is, and why people should be interested.

Video genres are still developing as more and more of the world turns to videos for various reasons, from education to marketing to entertainment. However, some common genres include marketing, education, how-to, music video, webcam rants, and storytelling.

Why is defining your video's identity so important? One of the most obvious reasons is so your video can be found. Take

YouTube, for instance. When uploading a video, you have the option to select a category for your video. When people search the platform for videos, your video will fall under the category related to what they're searching for, and it has a better chance of being found.

The second reason labeling your video with a specific genre is essential is that it allows you to build a framework. Each genre has a set of expectations. If those expectations aren't met, your viewers are going to walk away unhappy and unlikely to watch any other videos you make. Defining the genre will give you insight into what expectations you need to meet.

Let's go back to that horror and marketing film comparison we used earlier. To build a good horror movie plot, you need:

- Character introduction and a bit of background – not much but just enough to make them relatable to viewers
- A calm beginning that leads into setting the stage of where the horrors are to take place – often part of the character introduction
- An up and down yo-yo of fear and relief throughout that ultimately builds into a crescendo
- A dramatic ending that leaves a lingering heebie-jeebies feeling after the lights are turned back on

Now, for a good marketing video, you're going to need to fulfill completely different expectations:

- Introduction to the brand/product
- What the brand/product does
- Why the viewer absolutely needs the brand/product
- Why the brand/product is the right choice above competitors

We can then see that videos of different genres need to meet completely different expectations to satisfy audiences. Happy viewers are more likely to come back for more. That's why successful movie franchises can bring out several sequels; they get it right the first time, and they keep getting it right.

Intent

Do you want to attract new customers? Perhaps your aim is to showcase a new product or service. Do you want to educate people on a specific subject? Are you trying to grow the viewership of your social media channels or accounts? The identity or genre will already lead you to your intent, but it needs to be refined further. Be as detailed as possible when expressing what you want to achieve with your video.

Brainstorm intentions. Write down any and every purpose that pops into your head without judging whether it's really the intent or not. You can then narrow down your true intention from there.

For example,

Let's say you want to shoot a video for an animal shelter because they're in desperate need of funds to keep doing what they do. Your list of possible intentions may include:

- Raising loads of money
- Raising awareness around the dire situation of shelters being overburdened by the sheer number of unwanted animals.
- Showcasing how the shelter rehabilitates sick or abused animals for adoption
- Raising awareness of the importance of volunteers helping out
- Getting a news show to cover the shelter's story and the plight
- Showing where donated funds go within the shelter
- Informing viewers of the various services the shelter performs
- Impressing your audience with just how much work the shelter actually does
- Evoking emotion from your viewers for unwanted, abandoned, sick, and mistreated animals
- Making the audience feel they can make a difference by making contributions
- Showing the needs of the shelter and why they need help
- Showing viewers that happy endings are possible for adopted animals because of what the shelter does

Once you've drawn up a list of all the possible things you want your video to achieve, you can whittle it down to a single intention. Choosing one focal purpose will guide you through shooting it to have the most impact. Having too many intentions could end up watering the message down.

When choosing your intention, look for the ones that get your creativity firing on all cylinders by giving you lots of different ideas of how to portray the intent. For instance, you may decide you want to show your audience how the shelter rehabilitates sick or abused animals for adoption. This could lead you to shots of how ill or mistreated the animal is when it first arrives at the shelter, footage of the rehabilitation process, ending with shots that show how much the animal has recovered or changed when it's ready for adoption. See how focused your ideas become to stay on point with that specific intention?

Audience

Wouldn't it be fantastic if you could just make a video and absolutely everybody liked it? Unfortunately, like with most things, it's simply not that easy. Unless you're making a video to share with your family and friends, you're going to have a target audience you want the video to appeal to. To appeal to that particular group of people, you need to know who they are, what they want, and how to "push their buttons". How do you identify your target audience?

In a sense, you've already uncovered the first step to identifying your target audience. Your video's identity will already narrow it down. Horror movies appeal to horror movie fans. Marketing videos will appeal to those interested in your brand, products, or services. Educational and how-to videos will appeal to people who want to learn something. How you label your video will automatically eliminate everyone you don't want to appeal to.

Think about this: Sometimes, your video may even appeal to people who aren't actively interested in it until they get a whiff of it. Think about how many times you have become curious about a brand, product, or service you weren't interested in previously just because you saw an excellent video promoting it. Think about how many times you've been drawn into watching an ad on YouTube, for instance, because it was so good you wanted to see what it was all about instead of clicking that skip button as fast as possible.

Here's the trickier part, though. After you've determined your video's identity, you still need to dig deeper because you now only have a vague idea of who your video is meant for. To further refine your target audience, consider the following:

- Gender
- Age
- Location (local, national, international, as well as specific features regarding their site)
- Education level
- Economic bracket/income level and spending power (Do they have money of their own, and how much

can/do they spend on your type of products/services?)

- Social status
- Occupation
- The kinds of interpersonal relationships they have
- The social media platforms they prefer using
- The media (other than social media) platforms they prefer using
- The types of media they prefer accessing (text, images, video, etc.)

Create a target audience persona based on these key indicators to narrow down your video targets. Refining your audience creates a clearer path to success because you will hit all their key expectation points.

Your target audience isn't only restricted to the criteria above. You also need to know the answer to a very pertinent question. What device is your target audience most likely to use to watch your video? To figure this out, you can look at their age, how prevalent social media use is among that age group, and their lifestyle.

Age will give you a better idea of how likely they are to use social media, how much they're probably using it, and what social media platforms they prefer.

Their lifestyle will indicate whether they use computers or mobile devices more often. A busy person who isn't bound to a desk for hours every day is more likely to opt for mobile devices, such as mobile phones, to watch videos, while desk jockeys have constant access to a computer.

Why does the type of device your audience is using matter? Different shots look entirely different depending on the screen size you're watching it on. For instance, wider shots look better on larger screens where you can see more of the detail in the shot. It's the same with footage that has lots of detail. A small screen often causes the elements to shrink away into indiscernible nothingness, detracting from your video. Considering this aspect will help you make the most of each shot, so your viewers see everything you want them to see and don't miss out on essential details because their screen is too small to see them correctly.

Tip: Check out your competition. You can gain invaluable insight from scoping your competitors and taking stock of what they are doing and how they are doing. Sure, you don't want to be a copycat and make the same videos; you want to stand out. Watching successful videos in the same genre and with the same intention and audience shows you what your target audience wants and likes. Reading reviews and comments is a crucial part of your video reconnaissance. In the comments and reviews, you will discover what your target audience likes about competitor videos, what they want to see more of, what they would have liked done differently, and what they didn't like. Gathering this intel will steer you toward giving your viewers what they want and help you make even better videos than your competition.

MEASURABLE

How will you measure your video's success once you've made it and put it out there? The metrics you use to figure out how well your video is doing will depend on its specific purpose. What do you want your video to achieve? Identity and purpose differ in that videos with the same identity or genre can have different purposes. If you are making a how-to video, why are you making that video? If you are making a marketing video, why are you making that marketing video?

Here are metrics often used to measure a video's success:

Views: How many times a video is viewed is a good indicator of how many people it's reaching. The more views your video gets, the bigger your audience for that specific project.

Play rate: How many people who landed on your web page clicked that play button? If your page visitor to video play rate isn't great, perhaps your video doesn't have the ideal positioning. It may also indicate that page visitors prefer that content in text or image format. If your video isn't getting the expected play rate, try the following:

- Reposition the video to a more prominent spot on the page or to a different page altogether where it may be more helpful or appropriate.
- Make the embedded video window bigger to be more visible.

- Change the thumbnail to be more appealing or spark more interest.
- Reword the text around the video to clearly tell visitors what it's about or be catchier to pique their interest.

Play completion: How many people are watching the video right to the end? Are viewers losing interest and leaving part-way through? This could be happening for different reasons, including

- Poor visual or sound quality (or both)
- Lack of clarity regarding the topic
- The video goes off-topic
- The content is boring and not engaging enough to keep viewers' attention
- It's too long

Repeat plays: These could indicate that the content is engaging and entertaining when people watch it more than once.

Likes, follows, and channel subscriptions: As insignificant as the action of clicking the like button may seem, it's a conscious, specific, and deliberate action. The same goes for clicking the follow or channel subscription buttons. Getting likes means people genuinely like your video(s), which tells you you're doing something right. When they take the time to subscribe to your video channel, you can be sure you're doing something VERY right.

Comments: Engagement can be measured in many ways, from whether people are sticking around to watch the whole video to if they are sharing your video. An essential aspect of gauging the success of your video is to look at the comments it garners. Are you getting any comments at all? What kinds of comments are you getting; are they negative? Are they a simple "I really like your video."? Are people asking you/your channel/your other viewers questions? The amount and types of comments your video receives can indicate if you're on the right track or whether you fell off the wagon with that one.

Social media: Social media is today's equivalent of word-of-mouth. Is your video getting those online tongues wagging and recommendations in the form of shares? What are they saying? It doesn't help if people are talking if they're saying all the wrong things. If there are some negative mentions, look into them to improve your videos going forward.

Subscriptions and sales: Have you seen an increase in people signing up for your mailing list, buying into your subscription, or purchasing your products or services since using a video to boost your marketing?

Site metrics: What are your site metrics telling you, whether you are using a video posted directly onto your web page or another platform with a link back to your website? Are you seeing an increase in visitors to the video's page? Are you getting an increase in site or page visits? If the video is on your web page itself, are people sticking around on the page longer now that it has a video on it compared to when it was just text? Are visitors landing on the page your video is on and then exploring other pages on your website?

When using metrics to measure video success, you need a value to measure. Do you only want 1 view of your video, or do you want 100 or 10,000? Do you want 1 person to subscribe or make a purchase or 5, 15, or 30? Set a realistic goal for increases in metric measurements and use those goals as a yardstick for video success.

Important note: If you are using video to grow your brand, take stock of your metrics before you post your video so you have something to compare the new figures to after you put it out there.

ACHIEVABLE

Any new idea is exciting; it's easy to get swept up in your enthusiasm and lose sight of what is achievable. You need to determine whether you have the necessary motivation, dedication, and time to complete a video project. You can have all the resources in the world, but if you don't have those three crucial elements, your video will never see the light of online day. If you do have those three elements, it's time to look at your physical and monetary resources.

Not having the resources for specific aspects of a video doesn't necessarily mean you have to shelve the idea. Thinking outside the box, getting creative, and even compromising is the way to go.

Another aspect you need to keep realistic is the metric goals set out above. It's unrealistic to expect your very first video to go viral, double subscriptions, or triple sales. Set attainable goals for what you want your video to achieve.

RELEVANT

You can have the most impressive ideas for filming your video but are they relevant? They need to be aligned with your video's identity/genre, the topic of your video, and your audience and what they want/expect.

TIME-BOUND

You could spend months stuck in the planning phase or even take years to finish your video project if you don't set time limits to your goals. Goals give you a schedule to work with instead of letting procrastination get the better of you, and they help buoy your motivation. However, your time limits need to be just as realistic and achievable as the goals themselves. Don't take too long and let your video project die a slow death, but, at the same time, don't rush it.

BOTTOM LINE

Goal-setting is an essential step in the process of planning and preparing to shoot your video. The following steps can be measured up against your goals. Your budget and goals will ultimately influence how you develop the ideas for your video. The next chapter deals with creating your video content. It's a necessary step to take before you can start setting your stage. You can begin deciding what equipment you need to turn your vision into a reality when you have clear goals.

6

BRAINSTORMING

Once you have your budget pinned down and your video-making goals set, you can begin the brainstorming process in the pre-filming preparation. Brainstorming is coming up with a bunch of ideas. It doesn't mean only coming up with ideas you think are good. It means keeping an open mind and writing down every single thought that pops into your head without judgment. Any time you discard an idea without writing it down, you toss the potential to develop other ideas, essentially stemming your creative flow. How often have you found yourself saying, "I've got it! What about...Nah, never mind. It wouldn't work anyway."? That's not brainstorming.

It doesn't matter how far-fetched or implausible an idea seems; keep track of absolutely everything. You never know when something that seems crazy might get your synapses firing to come up with something more doable. Your mind is incredibly complex and wondrous and meticulously works in the background to find a solution to make an idea work by adapting the concept.

Brainstorming can take anywhere from a few minutes to several days. As long as you're still coming up with ideas, you need to be writing them down. Once you've come up with a decent stack of ideas, it's time to move on to the second phase of brainstorming. You now need to start making decisions about the ideas you've come up with. Pick all the ideas that stand out to you on the first run-through, even if they seem a little out-of-reach. Once you've made that list of possibilities, go through it again and pick only those ideas that you really like.

Remember, this narrowed-down list is still just a list of ideas. You may or may not use all of them, so don't restrict yourself to only ideas you are a hundred percent certain you definitely will use; it's often down to trial and error.

Tip: Physically write down your ideas using pen and paper. The brainpower and coordination involved in writing something down allow you to remember it better. It really makes it stick in your mind, which is what you want to happen when you want to give your mind time to tick over and come up with an alternative.

BOTTOM LINE

You can't start developing your video script without ideas, and those ideas only come from brainstorming. During the brainstorming stage, you explore any and all ideas, and by exploring all ideas, no matter how far-fetched, you're able to come up with doable alternatives that may work even better. You might think you have an idea of what you want to do. Comparing what's possible with your goals will help you narrow down options for what you actually need and not just what you think you want.

7

WRITING YOUR STORY AND SCRIPT

"No matter what you do. Your job is to tell a story."

–Gary Vaynerchuk

The terms 'story' and 'script' can sometimes be used interchangeably. The thing is, they're not one and the same. The story refers to the plot or what the video is about. You can use the components of storytelling to create a plot for your project to get you started. This helps lay the groundwork for the visual side of your video. The script is the verbal dialogue. Writing your script will help you refine your visual content to make it more impactful and structure your verbal content.

STORY FIRST

You can't write a script without knowing what your story is. Think about how you would describe a movie to someone. You'd usually start with, "It's about..." and not something like, "It has really great actors." Great actors and special effects don't tell a story. Without a story, most video falls flat.

Let's revisit that example of making a video about an animal shelter. Your intent will inspire your story, and the intent is to show your audience how the sanctuary rehabilitates sick or abused animals for adoption. You know what you want the video to achieve and how you can build a story around it. There are four elements you need to include in making that story:

A hero or subject: This is the star of your video. Your hero can be a person, animal, or even an object. The hero is the main focus of your video. In the case of the animal shelter video, you'd choose the animals being treated, rehabilitated, and adopted.

Beginning: This is the introduction to your story. Usually, the beginning introduces your hero, sets the scene for where they are, and gives the viewer an idea of the story's direction. If you don't hook your viewers within the first five seconds of watching, you can forget about them sticking around to find out more. Five seconds isn't a long time, so you need to make those first seconds count. It doesn't have to be complicated. Keep it simple but make it impactful. For example, you could open your shelter video with a neglected and terrified animal being unloaded from a vehicle and taken into the building. It's simple, it introduces your hero, shows where the story is taking place, hints at where the plot is going, and tweaks your audience's heartstrings, so they want to keep watching to find out what happens.

Middle: The middle is the meat of your video, where your story is told. The middle has to flow logically from the beginning and the end. In this case, you may want to use some shots of the neglected animal being cleaned up and given medical treatment. You may even want to chronicle the rehabilitation process. How much you pack into the middle of your video depends on how long it will be and what you want to include.

End: The end is there to leave your audience with a lasting impression once they've finished watching. It typically rounds out the video, bringing it neatly to a close. For the shelter video, viewers want to know what happens to the animal. If you leave them hanging there and simply end with a call to action to donate, viewers are going to be very annoyed because they haven't been given closure, and they're still wondering what happened next. You may end your video with a shot of the animal looking happy as can be and being adopted into a new home.

Important note: If you think something like a how-to or educational video doesn't need a story, think again. You still have to set out the flow of the information you're presenting to viewers, and that flow of information becomes your story or plot. Develop your story for these kinds of videos by writing down step-by-step what you will be telling your audience.

SCRIPT SECOND

Once you have your story flow in place, it's time to write your script. You need to ask yourself a few questions before actually starting to write your script.

Questions To Consider

Who is your audience? – You need to cater to your audience in terms of tone of voice, whether you speak more casually or professionally, phrases and language used, etc. You can also use this question to refine what kind of visual content you should use to tell your story; for example, animation/puppets/child actors are likely to appeal to children, while live-action/adult actors appeal to adults.

What do your viewers want or need? – This one is aimed explicitly at videos used to promote brands/products/services or educate viewers on a subject. Your script needs to address what your audience wants or needs without overloading them with wordiness or too much information. Pick one particular need to focus on instead of addressing all their needs at once.

What message do you want to send to viewers? – Don't just think about what you want to tell your audience. Think about what you want them to remember. This usually directly and clearly addresses the need you identified in the previous question.

What emotions do you want your viewers to feel? – Emotions are compelling and affect how people think and act. If your video promotes your brand/product/service to solve a problem, you want to make your audience feel understood and cared about. If you want your audience to get involved with something, you want to stir up emotions that will make them spring into action.

What action do you want viewers to take after watching your video? – Many videos include a call to action. Do you want viewers to buy your product, support a cause, subscribe to your channel, sign up for your e-course, etc.? Knowing what you want them to do will help you work that call of action into your video to increase the number of viewers who take the desired action.

Steps For Writing a Brief

Having answered these questions, you can now get down to the business of writing your script in a few simple steps:

Write a brief: Your brief is your jumping-off point. You may be thinking, "But, haven't we already gone over all of this?". Yes, but now it's time to put it together to support writing a compelling script. This is what to include in your brief:

- The identity/genre of your video
- Your video intent or goal
- What your video is about

- Who your target audience is
- What your main takeaways are for viewers
- What your call to action is
- What devices your audience will view the video on

Write your story outline: Use your brief and story concept to write down a detailed outline for your video. Write the summary in as much detail as you can and even extra optional ideas you may want to use.

Even though you've written an outline, don't restrict yourself to being inflexible when it comes to filming. You may find your original idea doesn't work as well as you thought it did, and those optional extra concepts could come in super handy.

Write your script in sections: Write scripts for each section of your video. This can be according to the beginning, middle, and end, or according to the different shots you want to use.

Support A-roll and B-roll: A-roll refers to your main shot, the one you want to be focusing on. B-roll refers to any footage you may want to supplement the A-roll with. For instance, if you make a product demonstration video, you may want your main footage to be a wider shot of the demonstrator working with the product. That will be your A-roll. Your B-roll may be made up of close-up shots of the demonstrator pushing buttons or showing off product details. You may cut from the wider shot to the closer shots, and when you intend to do this, you should write it into your script.

TIPS AND TRICKS

You can write a script using a few simple steps, but we're going to let you in on some tips and tricks for writing a great script to form the basis of an awesome video.

Keep it short: Our world is one of instant gratification. People want what they want and want it in the shortest time possible. Write a detailed script for any video but keep your actual video length as short and to the point as you can.

To keep your script concise but still make an impact, you should:

- Ditch the big words in favor of the language your audience uses every day.
- Say something different from what all your competitors are saying.
- Avoid repetition unless you're using it for dramatic effect.
- Leave out any information or visuals that aren't absolutely necessary.

Benefits of shorter videos include:

- Viewers are more likely to watch the whole thing without losing interest.

- Shorter videos have a faster pace, keeping viewers interested.
- Shorter videos = less planning = less time and effort.
- Shorter videos are generally cheaper to produce.

Think in shots: Shots can also be called cuts. Whatever video you're making, you want to avoid a static video of one continuous shot. Tell your story using different shots to compress time and keep it visually interesting. Using shots can also get your audience thinking which helps hold their attention. An example of shortening time and getting your audience thinking could be:

1. A shot of a child's mischievous face as their eyes shift to the left.
2. A shot of a cookie jar on a counter.
3. A shot of the same child looking over their shoulder to the right.
4. A shot of an adult (a parent) with their back turned toward the camera while talking on the phone.

These shots are all seemingly unrelated until you put them all together. You aren't moving the camera from the child's face to the cookie jar to the parent on the phone. Each shot only needs to last one or two seconds. You're creating interest by using different shots and making the audience think that they aren't spoon-fed, that the child wants a cookie but are engaging their brains and drawing the conclusion.

Use a storyboard: A storyboard is a set of still images or drawings, each representing a shot in the video, organized into a sequence. It's like a comic strip of your video. A storyboard allows you to pre-visualize your video. It's a powerful tool to help you plan aspects of filming, such as positioning, camera angles, effects, etc. Not only can you plan your shot beforehand, but you can also use the storyboard images to remind you of what you had in mind for the shot when you get around to actually filming it. It can also be useful for anticipating potential problems and coming up with solutions or realizing the shot may not quite work and coming up with a backup plan.

Read your script out loud: Reading your script aloud before you start filming has a variety of benefits:

- Finding where emphasis and inflection need to be placed for effect
- Pinpointing any awkward phrases or words
- Familiarizing you with your script, so you sound more natural and less stiff
- Getting an idea of how long it will take to work through the script

You can read your script aloud, record it, play it back and listen to your tone, speed of speech, inflection, etc. and decide where you need to put in some more work.

BOTTOM LINE

When you write a detailed script for your video, you build on your brainstorming process. You can develop new ideas, you can plan for setbacks, and you can really bring your video to life before you start filming. With a well-written script, you have an exact idea of what you are looking for when you start setting your stage. It's essential to create a script that is as detailed as possible so you can look at every aspect of your stage during the next planning phase. A poorly written script will leave you vulnerable to oversights, obstacles, and even failure.

PART III

CREATING YOUR STAGE

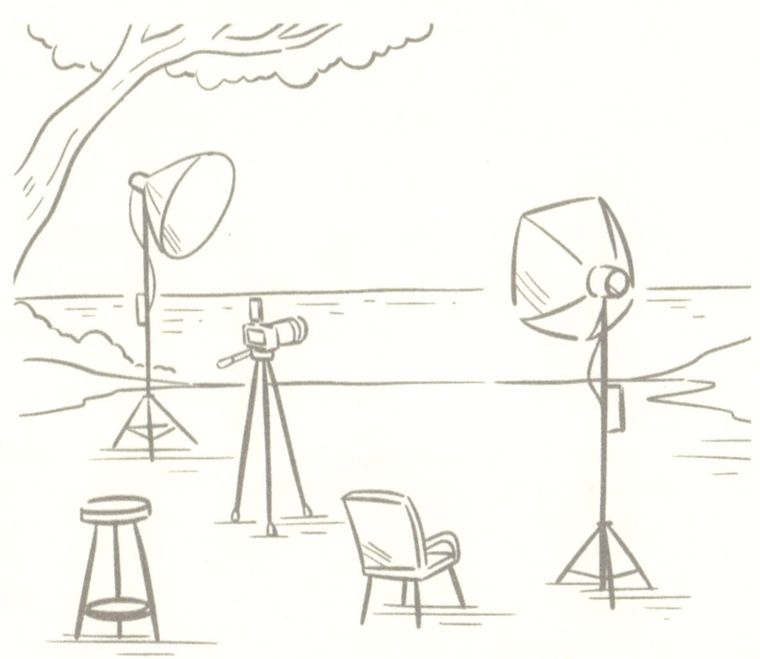

8

LOCATION

"It's all about location."

–Stephany Sofos

Many of the elements of your stage could come from your location. The problem is you may not always get to choose your location. Sometimes it's picked by someone else, such as your bride and groom for wedding videos or your boss for work-related videos. You need to know how to work with locations you have no say in, and those you can choose yourself.

LOCATIONS PICKED BY OTHERS

This can be tricky. You may envision a fantastic scene for your video, but what you actually get could be the complete opposite. This is where some scene sleuthing comes in, and a touch of creativity can go a long way. Here are some tips to draw the best out of the scene:

Look for attractive backgrounds at the location: The first thing to do when you're given a less-than-ideal site is to look for the most gorgeous environments. Try to find a few areas at the location you can work with.

Use props, if possible: You can make your location more aesthetically pleasing by using props like products, hanging a curtain, placing branding over a crack in the wall, etc.

Shift focus from important but ugly location elements: Sometimes, an unattractive feature of the location could be significant. Let's say you're shooting a wedding. The ceremony building is usually quite crucial for context but could be a monstrosity to look at. If you absolutely must have an ugly element in your shot, try removing the focus from the eyesore. Perhaps a stunning old oak tree on the grounds can dominate the frame, with the ceremony building still visible in the background but not taking center stage.

Take pictures: Take lots of photos of the location from every angle and at different times of day to have a visual record of what you're dealing with and the kind of natural light you'll get at various times of the day.

PICKING YOUR OWN LOCATION

Can you pick your own location to shoot your video? Great! What now? Here are some guidelines for choosing the right place for filming:

Scout locations in person: There are some amazing online resources to look for sites, such as Locations Hub and Shot Hotspot. However, avoid falling into the trap of relying on a digital impression of a location alone. We'll discuss the necessary considerations for choosing a location that you can only see in person in the following points.

Consider your script: Your script will play a significant role in deciding the location. The location must fit the story you want to tell and the script you're using.

Look for the elements you've written into your script: A sunny park might seem ideal, but if it doesn't have that crucial towering oak tree your hero proposes to his love under, you can't shoot the scene.

Does the location support what you're trying to convey to your audience? A burly, tattooed biker riding his Harley down a green, hilly country road with quaint farms tells an entirely different story to him riding down a crowded city street.

Look for light: You could always use artificial lighting. So, why should you look at lighting in a potential location, and what should you be looking for?

If you don't have additional artificial lighting equipment, but thought it necessary you'd have to hire some. Can you afford this additional expense, and more importantly, why would you want to shell out extra cash if you don't actually have to? Choosing a location with the proper lighting for your shoot saves you time and money.

What time of day are you going to be shooting? Does the natural light at that time of day suit your scene? Mellow afternoon sunshine filtering in through a window will look different from the crisp morning light you envisioned. What's the angle the light's coming from, and where are the shadows cast from nearby trees, buildings, etc.? The sun casts shadows in different directions as it moves across the sky, and the light will fall on your subject from different angles, possibly changing the appearance.

Consider sound: You may have the scripted narration in mind when you think about audio, but that's not all you need to be concerned about.

Listen to the ambient sound at the location, paying attention to the kinds of sounds you can hear and the volume. Will the volume of the ambient noise overpower your intended video audio or be distracting to viewers? What sounds can you hear that don't fit with your video? Even if you are shooting a video in your own home, listen to what you can hear at the time of day you want to film.

Interruptions and disruptions: Visit the potential location at the time of day you want to shoot your video.

What is happening at that time of the day? If you cannot control the location, you may encounter interruptions because of noise, people wandering through your shot, and so on.

What is happening around your location that could affect your filming? There could be a quaint building in the background when you start shooting, which could be demolished halfway through filming. Find out about anything that could be happening at and around the location that could cause disruptions.

Take a camera: Take lots of pictures of each location to compare locations. Pictures are a visual reminder of a location's good and bad points. They can also help you develop your script in more detail or make tweaks to fit the site better.

Additional considerations:

- Nearby airports – Airplanes taking off and landing could be a noise consideration
- Safety – What is the area like around the location? Is it safe?
- Access – Can you freely access the location, or do you need someone to give you access?
- Price – Is the location free or paid for? Does it fit into your budget, or can you find another place just as good at a lower price?
- Parking – Is there parking available? Is it close by? Is it safe? Is it free, or will it add to your costs?

- Set up and space – Does the location offer space for equipment and crew set up?
- Electricity – You may need electricity for equipment and lighting. Do you know where the breaker boxes are?
- Amenities – What amenities does the location offer, such as a bathroom and nearby shops?

FREE LOCATIONS

Who doesn't love getting something for free? Location hiring can chew into your budget. You may have the ideal location sitting right under your nose through connections like friends or family. Someone you know may have access to the perfect site – perhaps an apartment, a beautifully manicured garden or a field.

Something else to think about is striking up a partnership and collaborating with a location or business. This can be tricky in the wake of so many social media 'influencers' trying to get expensive freebies. Does appearing in your video offer them anything in return? How will they benefit from the exposure? If you can collaborate with a location, you could offer a trade by placing their products in your video.

Don't be afraid to ask if you can use the location for free but be careful not to take advantage of your connections. Credit them in the video credits, and be sure to say thank you.

Important note: Just because you can get a location for free doesn't mean you should use that location. The location sets the scene and shouldn't be chosen just because it's free, especially if it doesn't really fit your story and script.

BOTTOM LINE

You've developed ideas, and written your script, now you've decided on your location or, at least, you have a good idea of what to look for when choosing your site. In the next chapter, we'll explore what to look for in your background and foreground. You may have to revisit your locations to look at these crucial aspects, but knowing what to look for will help you make decisions. Before you start recording, every decision you make is a step in the right direction toward creating a better video.

9

BACKGROUND AND FOREGROUND

Hold on a moment, aren't the location, background, and foreground the same thing? Not quite. While your location can provide a backdrop and a foreground, not all sites provide a backdrop and a foreground suitable for your video. A point, in case, is an empty room with nothing more than four walls and maybe a window. Nobody enjoys looking at a blank wall, so you'll need to create a background. Backgrounds and foregrounds need special attention to detail, whether naturally occurring or created.

REAL VS. ARTIFICIAL

There are two major types of backgrounds to use in videos. You get real backgrounds and artificial backdrops. Whether you choose a real background or an artificial backdrop will come down to the kind of video you're making and what you want that video to look like.

What's a real background? A real background is any background that shows viewers where you are, giving the scene context. Think outdoor spaces, streets, offices, rooms, and so on.

What's an artificial backdrop? An artificial backdrop doesn't convey context, such as a blank wall, curtain, sheet of paper, or a green screen. You could also use a backdrop you've constructed, say, out of cardboard or foam, to give the scene behind the subject some character. The point of an artificial backdrop is that it isn't what is really in the background; it's "made up".

Artificial Backdrops

Artificial backdrops have a time and a place, but they should be used with caution. Here are the pros and cons of using a fake background.

Pros:

- No location hire is required, saving you time and money
- It's entirely within your control; you decide color, texture, design, etc.
- You can set up your 'stage' anywhere, and your audience will never be able to guess you're in your untidy bedroom.

- Its clean simplicity can lend your video a professional look.
- The focus is placed on the person speaking to the camera.
- Using the same background for all your videos creates consistency.
- It can be used many times over without incurring additional expenses.

Cons:

- It doesn't convey context to where you are, which risks giving your video a detached and unrelatable feeling.
- It can create a boring video with no visual interest aside from the person speaking to the camera.

Real Backdrops

Just as with artificial backgrounds, real backgrounds have their uses for specific types of video. Let's look at why you would and wouldn't, want to use a real backdrop.

Pros:

- It gives your video a more personal feel, possibly making you seem more relatable to your audience.
- It can showcase your personality.
- It's visually attractive.

- You can use lenses and settings to blur the background when using a DSLR or mirrorless camera. This means viewers don't get hung up looking at the details.
- It can be cost-effective if you're using your own bedroom or a room in your own home.
- It tells your audience where you are, giving your video visual context.
- It can drive your message home to your viewers.

Cons:

- A busy background with a lot of movement or clutter can distract viewers from the speaker.
- Location hire can be costly.
- It could create inconsistencies if items/furniture are moved around.

DOS AND DON'TS

Whether you are using an artificial or a real background, there are a few things you should do and some you should avoid when deciding on, creating, and setting up your background.

Dos:

Make it relevant. Backgrounds need to fit the type of video you're making and the script. You're going to shoot outdoors if you're making a gardening video, not sitting on your sofa. Suppose your video is about an affluent character. In that case, you'll want to use an upscale apartment or high-end car in a classy neighborhood. You won't want a studio apartment downtown above a take-out restaurant with a shabby old car parked in the alleyway.

Match the speaker's wardrobe to the background. Whether it's an artificial background or a real background, avoid color and pattern clashes between the environment and the speaker's wardrobe. For instance, you don't want to be wearing a purple sweater against a yellow background. Being complementary colors, they will make each other stand out. You also don't want to be wearing a striped shirt on a sofa with oversized zig-zag patterned cushions. You get the idea.

Blur a real background if the finer details aren't crucial to the video. Blurring the background helps focus the viewer's attention on the speaker.

Use a solid, smooth sheet of paper or material for multiple interviews in front of the same backdrop. A solid, seamless background will make cutting between shots smoother.

When using a real background, switch up the angles to show each interviewee in front of a different view of the room.

Use multiple lights and diffusers when shooting in front of a whiteboard. Whiteboards are notorious for bouncing light back in reflections. (We'll discuss lighting in more depth in a bit!)

Pay attention to the little details. A single piece of litter on the ground, a coffee spill down the side of a mug, skewed wall art, and many other details could become a distraction or look unappealing.

Take some test shots. Test shots are the only way to really see what the camera sees and how your 'stage' looks from behind the lens, which is where your audience will be watching from.

Have the same or similar colors in several accessories in your shot. Just a few points of similarity in color and even pattern or texture can help bring a sense of consistency to the scene.

Use subtle product or branding placement in your scene. You're going to want to aim for subtle suggestions instead of in-your-face branding. This is especially useful for collaboration videos. Keep it simple, keep it subtle, and make it strategic, so your audience sees the branding but it doesn't become the video's focus.

Don'ts:

Don't use bright colors, fussy patterns, or cluttered backgrounds. You want to focus on the speaker and not the environment. Bright colors can reflect their color onto the speaker and surroundings. Fussy patterns can be distracting or even downright unpleasant to look at. Cluttered backgrounds draw the viewer's eye away from the speaker to the clutter instead.

Don't switch up colors for colored artificial backdrops. Keep the color of your artificial backdrop consistent. There are times and places to break any rule for specific types or emphasis in videos. However, if in doubt, leave the additional colors out.

Don't rely on ambient light alone for shots of the same scene at different times of the day. Ambient light can change. A cloud could come over the sun. The sun moves, and so do shadows. The brightness of natural ambient light can change at the drop of a hat. Create consistency by employing additional artificial lighting techniques. If you can only use ambient lighting, plan to shoot on cloudy days for more consistent natural light.

Don't include any unnecessary props or details. A natural background can be dynamic and exciting, but it can also become cluttered and overwhelming. Are there unimportant items in your shot? Get rid of them.

BOTTOM LINE

It's not just about focusing on your subject during a shoot. Your background and foreground can have a considerable impact. Your foreground and background can actually make or break whether your subject commands your audience's attention. Foregrounds and backgrounds can also be used for subtle marketing by sending subliminal visual messages to your audience.

However, foreground and background aren't the only factors you need to consider when deciding on a location. You can have the perfect setting, but your ideal environment is all for naught if the light is terrible. Let's get into lighting to help you make the best decision about location.

10

LIGHTING

We touched on lighting in the previous chapter; now it's time to better understand light and its importance in creating a video that looks more professional. We've said it before, video, like still photography, is the art of capturing light. If there is no light, you're not going to have an image, but it's not as simple as that. Let's look at the role good lighting plays in making a video.

THE IMPORTANCE OF LIGHTING

"The secret to life is putting yourself in the right lighting."

–Susan Cain

- Proper lighting makes a video look more professional. One of the visual elements that scream,

"I don't know what I'm doing, but I'm making a video anyway", is poor lighting.

- Good lighting allows viewers to see detail. Whether your scene is too dark or you have reflections bouncing off surfaces, incorrect lighting means your audience is likely to miss out on essential information. This could include color, demonstration techniques, or writing.
- Lighting highlights what you want to showcase. When used correctly, light can draw the viewer's eye to the part of the scene you want them to focus on.
- Light can set the mood of a scene. Bright light is cheerful and safe, while gloomy scenes are ominous and dangerous. Mellow lighting conveys relaxation, contentedness, and maybe even a hint of laziness. In this way, how a scene is lit can influence how a viewer feels while watching the video.
- Light paints a picture of your character's mental and emotional state. The harshness, color, angle, and even size of the light can change how your audience perceives your character.

There are two sources of light you can use when making a video:

Natural light: As the name implies, this is all-natural, and there are no plugs, wires, or bulbs involved aside from the great big bulb in the sky. The sun's light filters through to create soft natural light, even on overcast days.

Artificial light: This kind of light is created using electricity. It can be manipulated subtly or, to a crazy extent, to achieve the lighting you want for your video with the right equipment.

BASIC LIGHTING TECHNIQUES

We'll get into the details of using both natural and artificial lighting in a moment, but before we get to that, let's take a moment to discuss lighting techniques. The following basic methods can employ natural or artificial light, and some-times even both!

Key light: This is the main light source for your scene. It is the strongest light illuminating your subject, and it's often positioned at an angle in front of the subject. This creates shadows, but that's what fill lights and reflectors are for.

Fill light: Your key light is the strongest and can create deep shadows. Fill lights are not as strong and are positioned to lighten harsh shadows to bring out details that would other-wise be lost.

Side lighting: As the name suggests, this is lighting that hits your subject from the side so that one side is lit up while the other is darker with shadow.

Backlight: The subject is lit up from behind. The light faces the camera and can be used for two effects. On the one hand, the light can be softer and lend the subject a slight glow. On the other hand, the light can be harsher to create more of a silhouette, with the front of the subject in deep shadow with little to no detail.

Soft light: This light can be bright but balanced, so it doesn't create any harsh contrasts between shadows and light areas. The subject is lit overall and fairly evenly.

Hard light: The light is harsh and creates deep shadows contrasting with bright sections. This technique can create moody shots or highlight a subject brightly.

Low-key light: There are many shadows, and the light is more likely to be weaker and not very bright.

High-key light: Intensely bright light is used to almost over-light the subject, so there are next to no shadows in the scene.

Bounce light: Strong, bright light can't always be aimed directly at the subject. Instead, a reflector is used to bounce the light toward the subject. The light is then spread over a wider area, which diffuses the harshness.

Practical light: Any source of light that can be seen in the shot, such as lamps and other light fixtures, televisions, candles, or pretty much anything that produces light and is visible to the viewer. More often than not, practical lights don't give off enough light to illuminate the subject on their own but help create an ambiance. On the other hand, if you're making a video showcasing studio photography, you may have bright studio lights in your shot.

HARD AND SOFT LIGHT

Most of your lighting will be either hard or soft light. Many other lighting techniques rely on these two kinds of light, so it's pretty important to understand why, how, and when to use them.

Hard Light

Before we explain what hard light is, we need to explain how it's described. Hard light is the photographic and video term for light that is harsh. The harshness of the light is necessary to create the effects described below. So, to clarify, we'll be using the terms hard and harsh interchangeably.

You have lit-up areas and lots of shadows. Side lighting is often used to create hard light, but it can also come from behind or directly in front. You're generally emphasizing shadows for dramatic effect or separating your subject from a dark background.

The trade-off when using hard light is that imperfections are brought to light, so to speak. Think skin imperfections like wrinkles and spots if you're shooting a close-up headshot. For the most part, it's not a flattering light to use if you're going to be close to the camera and aren't looking to create an edgy look.

When should you use hard light?

- Focusing on creating shadows as opposed to balanced lighting

- Creating a dramatic, dangerous, intense, or mysterious look and feel to the shot
- Separating your subject from the background
- Filming in black and white (hard light isn't strictly necessary for black and white but it helps create contrasty shadows)

How do you create hard light?

- Use a light source with a smaller surface area to limit how much the light spreads out.
- Use a light that doesn't have any diffusing coverings on it, such as a softbox, and don't use any other diffusion techniques.
- Move a light further away from the subject. Less shadow will be filled in when the light is further away.
- Utilize harsh midday (or shortly on either side of midday) sunlight on a clear day.
- Position your subject in front of or to the side of a clear glass window when shooting indoors.

How can hard light separate a subject from the background?

The trick is to use a dark background, like black or deep shadow. From there, you can position the light directly in front of the subject to illuminate it brightly from the front, creating that separation. This may work well for products and props (providing they don't have any imperfections) but not for people. Alternatively, you can position the light at an angle from the side or even from the back. Hence, it high-lights the subject's edges instead of letting them melt into the background. When used on people, this side or backlighting often highlights the person's hair and is called hair lighting.

Soft Light

Soft light is balanced to reduce shadows and harsh contrasts. It's much more flattering than hard light and can soften the appearance of imperfections. The light will come from various directions to cancel out or lighten shadows for a softer look. Unlike the drama of hard light, which can create a darker mood, soft light helps portray a happier mood and even innocence.

Soft light is often preferred for almost every shot, from land-scapes to headshots. It's, dare we say, more wholesome and flattering to many types of subjects.

When should you use soft light?

- Interviews, tutorials, demonstrations, documentaries, and pretty much any shot you can think of
- Shots that don't need a dramatic or moody feel and look
- Filming in black and white (black and white can be beautifully used with both hard and soft light)
- Portraying your subject or scene as neutral, meaning it doesn't evoke strong emotions and doesn't come

across as good or bad, menacing or particularly friendly/cheerful, and so on.

How do you create soft light?

- Use a light source that's larger in relation to your subject. A bigger light source spreads the light out more.
- Position the light closer to your subject to spread it more evenly across it.
- Use diffusion techniques such as softboxes or light shining through a filtering material, like gauze.
- Whether filming indoors or outdoors, use bounce lighting techniques to reflect more light onto various subject angles.
- Hang near-clear material in front of a window to create soft natural light indoors.
- Film outdoors during the golden hours (the hour after sunrise or before sunset) or on overcast days where the clouds act as natural diffusion filters.

NATURAL LIGHT

Let's start off with natural light because it's usually readily available, can be cost-effective, and is often considered the most beautiful kind of light. What are the natural lighting pros and cons for making videos?

Pros:

- It's readily available during daylight hours
- Little to no equipment is necessary
- It's cost-effective
- No electricity is needed
- There's variability between harsh and soft lighting
- There are variable light color hues (the afternoon sun has a different color to the morning sun, and sunny days have a different color to overcast days)

Cons:

- It's not available at night or in dark spaces
- The amount of natural light entering a space could be too little for proper lighting
- The variability in the strength and color can cause consistency problems due to different light at different times of the day or from one day to the next due to weather

Tips: Filming in Natural Light Outdoors

The great outdoors is where natural light is predominantly found. If you're planning on shooting outdoors, you need some know-how to make that beautiful natural light work for you instead of against you.

Don't shoot at midday: As we explained in the section on hard light, avoid filming under the midday sun.

Backlight with the sun: Avoid using the sun as your key light, whether intentionally or unintentionally. Position your subject so the sun is lighting them from behind. Having the sun in front of your subject will cause blown-out (overly bright) faces and squinting into the sun, which is never a good look for anybody.

Avoid direct backlighting with the sun: Wait, what? Didn't we just tell you to use the sun as a backlight? Yes, but the angle is crucial for success. Don't place your subject with the sun directly behind them, in line with them. Make sure the sun is behind them from an angle, otherwise, you'll end up with a featureless silhouette.

Don't get the sun in your shot: Avoid having the sun visible in your shot as it will create a blindingly white spot and flare, which, while arty, isn't a good idea for most videos.

Film during the blue and golden hours: hours after sunrise and before sunset are both golden hours (also known as 'magic hours'), when the light is redder and softer than at other times of the day. The light is crisp and gorgeous, but the sun hasn't reached its full harshness yet. There are also times known as the 'blue' hours. The blue hours are the hour before the sun rises and after it sets. There is still light to work with this time, but it's not harsh because the sun is no longer visible over the horizon.

Film night scenes during the blue hours: This is an excellent trick if you want to shoot a night-looking scene but don't have the lights and equipment to actually shoot at night. There is still enough ambient light to work with, so your subject is visible while making the background behind them look more like nighttime.

Use bounce light techniques: Try positioning your subject in lightly shaded areas and use reflectors to bounce the light toward them at an angle to illuminate the shadows.

Avoid sunglasses as much as possible: When you have a person speaking to your audience, you want them to make a connection with viewers. For that to happen, the audience needs to see their eyes. Position the subject so that they aren't facing directly into the sun.

However, if you simply HAVE to shoot in harsh light, have your subject wear sunglasses. If they're going to be squinting into the sun anyway, it's better to protect their eyes. Squinting is also distracting to the viewer and doesn't make your subject look good.

Find shade: If you have to shoot in bright sunlight and your location (and script) allows you to utilize a shaded area, go ahead. You can use bounce lighting techniques to lessen the shadows.

Watch out for strange shadows: Midday is the only time you'll have minimal shadows, but we know that's a terrible time of the day to do your filming. As the sun moves during the day, shadows not only shift but lengthen. Scout your location at different times of the day. Make notes of the shadows that are cast, their direction and length, and where you will be shooting to avoid weird shadows being cast over your subject.

Avoid dappled light: This one ties in with the shadow advice above. Dappled light may look charming with the sun peeking through the leaves and branches of trees, but it's not so lovely when your subject is mottled or has patchy shadows all over their face.

Shoot on cloudy days: Overcast days put a damper on the harshness of sunlight, allowing you to get a softer light that produces less shadow and contrast.

Rehearse and prepare ahead of time: The sun doesn't stop moving. If you plan to film at 10:00 a.m., make sure everything is appropriately set up and everyone is well-rehearsed before. You don't want to be setting up and rehearsing while you're losing that precious, perfect light you planned for your video.

Use nets to partially block light: Nets will help you lessen the amount of light reaching your subject without blocking it completely. They're useful for toning down the brightness and making it less harsh with lower-contrast shadows.

Use diffusers: If you're dealing with harsh light, you need to soften; use diffusers in the same way you would use flags to impede some of the light, spread it out, and soften it on your subject.

Tips: Filming in Natural Light Indoors

Just because you're shooting indoors doesn't necessarily mean you have to have a lighting kit to get decent lighting.

Windows and doors are excellent sources of natural light indoors. If you are shooting indoors, pick a location that offers you lots of natural light through windows. How do you use window lighting effectively?

Backlighting: This is where you need to tread very carefully. Placing your subject directly in front of a window, a light, or the sun is a huge no-go. All you'll get is a blown-out shot with a silhouette. Make sure the backlight is behind the subject at an angle.

Front lighting: Windows can illuminate your subject from the front. However, there are considerations. The sunlight shouldn't be shining directly into the window, blinding your subject or making them squint at the camera. Your subject may also not stand out from the background because the light coming into the window will light it just as evenly. You'd need to use additional backlighting to help make your subject stand out.

Key lighting: When the light streaming in through a window is bright and strong, you can use that light as your key light. This can be from any angle. Reflectors can bounce light back at your subject from another angle, or lighting equipment can be used to help fill in any shadows.

Diffusers and nets: Use diffusers and nets to control the amount and brightness of the light coming in through windows to avoid hard light and high-contrast shadows.

Shoot at midday: Yes, you read that right. Unlike outdoors, where the midday sun can be harsh and unforgiving, indoors it's a brilliant time of day for filming.

ARTIFICIAL LIGHT

Artificial lighting can be used indoors or outdoors. However, it's more commonly used indoors where there may not be enough natural light coming in. Artificial light sources are everything from studio lights to lamps, candles, and torches. They may be the only light source, or they could enhance the natural light you're already working with.

A Word on Light Color

Different types of light or different bulbs give off light of different colors. This variation is called the color temperature. Even natural light varies in color at different times and under different weather conditions.

The color of the light will tint everything it touches. Try holding a piece of red-colored cellophane up in front of a torch, shining the light onto a white surface, and observing how the light is red. The same principle applies. Now add mixed lighting into the equation. Mixed lighting happens when you have light sources with different color temperatures in the same scene, and it can get pretty complicated.

As someone who isn't making videos professionally, you don't have to worry too much about light color correction. DSLR and mirrorless cameras and most entry-level and prosumer video cameras will come with automatic white balance. Automatic what? White balance is the function in cameras that balances out the color temperature of the light so that white appears white and not tinted yellow or blue. When a white object in a scene seems white, everything else should appear in its natural color.

If the automatic white balance is outstanding and can do the job for you, why did we just spend time telling you about different light colors? It all comes down to mixed lighting. Automatic white balance is super helpful, but it's not infallible. To help your camera achieve the correct automatic white balance, always use artificial lights with the same color temperature.

Light color is measured in Kelvin (K) and ranges from 1,000 to 10,000, with 1,000 being the color of candlelight and 10,000 being the color of a clear, blue sky. The lower the Kelvin rating of light, the warmer or more yellow to red it is. The light will be cooler or more blue when the rating is higher. The packaging on lights should provide you with the color temperature of the light so you can pick out the same color for a multiple-light setup.

Here are some dos and don'ts to help your camera achieve the right white balance:

Dos:

- Ask the sales clerk what the color temperature of the lights is when buying them.

- Read the packaging on any lights or bulbs to ensure you are buying the same color temperature. Even the same type of lights, such as LEDs, come in different color temperatures, so you need to make sure you get the same color.
- Perform a test shot before filming. Set up your scene and lighting and record a short video to check that the whites are white and not tinted blue or yellow.

Don'ts:

- Use different types of light (such as halogen and fluorescent lights together) in the same scene if you can help it.

Try this: Even household light bulbs have different colors. The next time you're in the store, check out the packaging of different indoor and outdoor lights and take note of the different color temperatures available.

LIGHTING EQUIPMENT

Before you walk into your nearest photographic store and start pulling lighting kits off the shelf, you need to know what the different pieces of equipment are and what they do. It's pointless throwing money away on the equipment you don't need or won't use.

Stands: Light stands offer you versatility. A stand is your hands-free lighting buddy that can raise or lower your light and support additional modifiers like umbrellas. When purchasing a light stand, you have to know the weight of your light and what modifiers you will use. Choose a stand that can handle the weight of all of the equipment you may want to attach to it. Be careful not to opt for a light stand that can only just accommodate the full weight of your gear. Pick a stand that can handle a little more weight to be on the safe side.

Umbrellas: Umbrellas should be your go-to choice when you start using and trying to control artificial light. They're easier to use than softboxes. Umbrellas come in different sizes and materials, depending on what you're going to be using them for. You get shoot-through and reflective umbrellas. As the names imply:

- Shoot-through umbrellas are used to diffuse the light by placing them in front of the light source with the light source facing your subject.
- Reflective umbrellas are used with the light source facing away from your subject. Umbrellas bounce light back toward your subject, which will spread the light over a larger area but also make it less bright at the same time.

Shoot-through umbrellas are made of see-through white material. On the other hand, reflective umbrellas are made with a black outer and either a white or silver inner. Silver inners will reflect more light for brighter illumination than white inners.

When using umbrellas, it's important to remember a few key rules:

- The larger the reflective umbrella, the wider it will spread the light. The wider the area light spreads over, the less bright it will become toward the edges.
- The closer to the light source a reflective umbrella is, the more light it will reflect and the brighter it will be.
- The closer the light source and shoot-through umbrella are, the less the light will be diffused.

Softboxes: A softbox is used to shape, direct, and diffuse light. They offer you more control over your light, but that increased control means they are trickier to get the hang of than umbrellas. Softboxes come in various shapes and sizes, depending on your needs. The black exterior and white interior of a softbox mean you can shape the light according to the shape of the softbox and direct it more precisely than with an umbrella. Softboxes can even spread light. Their white interiors reflect the light within the 'box' to create a larger light source when the light leaves through the diffusion screen in the front.

Reflectors: Reflectors come in various shapes and sizes and are used to bounce light from the light source onto your subject. Reflectors can diffuse light, spread it, and create fill light. They come in white, gold, and silver. White reflectors bounce less light for a softer look, and gold/silver reflects more light, making it brighter. When would you use reflectors?

- To bounce natural light into a shaded area to make it brighter
- To reflect light onto a subject as a fill light to reduce shadows
- To reflect harsher light from the source onto the subject to soften the light
- To bounce light from a smaller light source onto the subject to light up a larger area

Tips for using reflectors:

- The closer the light source and reflector are, the less the reflected light will spread.
- The closer the light is to the reflector, the less it will be diffused.
- The closer the reflector and subject are, the more light it will bounce onto it.
- The closer the reflector is to the subject, the smaller the spread area.
- Silver reflectors will make the reflected light cooler (bluer).
- Gold reflectors will make the reflected light warmer (yellower).

Diffusers: Diffusers serve one purpose, softening harsh light by diffusing it through a see-through material. Diffusers can literally be made from thin white material (think of how voile curtains soften the light coming in through a window) to plastic sheets, to frosted glass.

Tips for using diffusers:

- Diffusers cannot spread light like an umbrella, softbox, or reflector does
- The closer the light source and the diffuser are, the less the light will be diffused
- Diffusers should be perfectly white; otherwise, they will add color to the light shining through them
- The thinner/less opaque the material you are using to diffuse light, the less the light will be softened

Lighting Setup

Lighting setup refers to the positioning of your lights. Depending on how many lights you have, you can use one-, two- or three-point lighting setups to create the ideal lighting for your video.

Tips

Imagine standing on a giant clock face when setting up lighting. Position your subject where you want it, and then make that position the 12 o'clock position of the clock face. You can then easily position your light sources according to the other hour positions in relation to your subject at 12 o'clock. We'll be doing this in the following explanations of lighting setups.

If you are working with a fixed light source that cannot be moved, imagine the giant clock face oriented according to where you want the light to be. You can then position your subject in the 12 o'clock position accordingly.

As a general rule, when lighting a subject from the side, you don't want to light it/them directly from the side. This will create harsher shadows on the side opposite to the light source. Instead, lighting setups usually light a subject diagonally from one side to lessen the shadows on the opposite side.

When positioning your lights, you will usually have multiple possible positions you can use that put the source diagonally side on to the subject. Whether you position the lights to the left or right, or more or less to the side, will depend on the subject and looks best on that particular person/thing. Play around to find the best position for that specific subject.

One-Point Lighting

One-point lighting makes use of only one light source. This could be natural light or artificial light. Ideally, you want to position this light at the subject's 4, 5, 7, or 8 o'clock with the camera at 6 o'clock. The preferable positioning would be at the four or eight o'clock position.

Ring light: A ring light is an alternative to a standard light for one-point lighting. However, there are a few things you need to consider. Ring lights provide relatively flat lighting, meaning they tend to light the face evenly, so there is very little shadow, if any at all. A ring light is usually covered with diffusion material which automatically softens the light. This soft, even lighting is why ring lights are also known as beauty lights.

Two-Point Lighting

You can position the lights at the 4 or 5 and 7 or 8 positions on the clock face for a two-point lighting setup. Again, the preferable positions would be the 4 or 8 o'clock positions. You can use lights of the same brightness or a brighter key light and dimmer fill light for this setup. If you are using lights of two different strengths, make sure you position the key light on your subject's "good side" to highlight the best angle to view them from and your fill light on the other side.

Tip: Using key and fill lights for this setup will give you more depth by creating soft shadows on the side of the fill light. Using two lights of equal brightness will create all-around even lighting, which will not cast shadows and flatten the scene out.

Three-Point Lighting

A three-point lighting setup is a traditional approach and the most favored setup for videos. It's easily adjustable and is ideal for a single person speaking to an audience. To create this lighting setup, position your key and fill lights on the clock face at the 4 or 5 and 7 or 8 o'clock positions. Use the key light to highlight the subject's best side. Position the background light at the 1, 2, 10, or 11 positions facing the back of the subject diagonally. The aim is to backlight the subject, so they glow and are separated from the background.

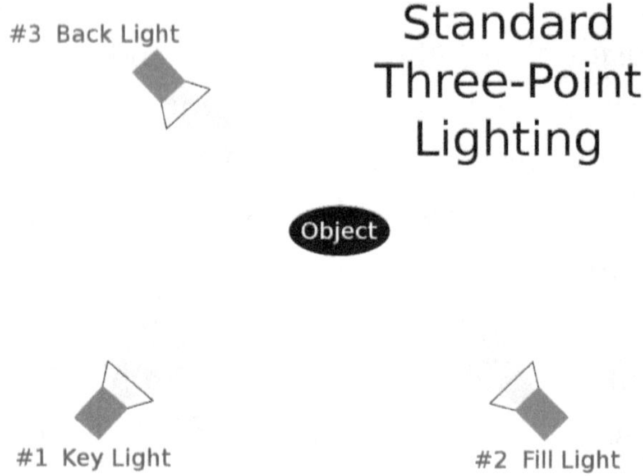

Tip: Try positioning your backlight at all the possible positions and swivel it slightly from side to side to work out which angle works the best for your shot.

BOTTOM LINE

Lighting is crucial to the visual quality of your video. Depending on your location, budget, and equipment, you can make pretty much any location work with artificial lighting. Suppose you don't have the equipment or budget to hire or buy it. In that case, you need to look for a location that offers you the natural lighting you need to properly illuminate your subject.

Alongside lighting, one more factor is vital for choosing the right location, and we're about to get into it in the next chapter. Your lighting can be a bit off, and your visual quality can be less than professional. However, if your audio sucks, you're likely to lose your audience's attention and not deliver your message to them effectively.

11

AUDIO

"In a world of audio and visual marvels, may words matter to you and be full of magic."

–Peter Godfrey-Smith

The era of silent films is a thing of the past. Audio is an integral part of modern video. In fact, it's probably more important than you realize. Audio can make or break your video, even if the visuals are excellent.

What does audio mean, exactly?

- Voice: You can either have a subject speaking directly to the camera, like in an interview, or you can have a voice-over.

- Sound effects: Just about anything can be a sound effect, from a crash to the hum of a coffee shop to the screeching of car tires on the road.
- Music: Music can be on-screen, filmed with the subject and heard by them, or it can be a "music over" like a voice-over which the subject cannot hear but the audience can.

What does audio bring to a video?

Information: If you are not telling a story in visuals, audio is the only way you will convey the information you want your audience to receive. This can be in an interview, a lecture, or an educational or how-to video. Suppose your audience can't hear what you are telling them. In that case, they won't get the information they want and will probably look for another video that will give them what they want.

Atmosphere: Atmosphere could mean the sounds surrounding your subject that tell your audience where they are. For instance, atmospheric audio may be the bustling hubbub of a city street, the stillness of the countryside broken only by the noises made by birds and other animals, or the clicking of keyboards, hum of technology, and ringing of phones in an office.

Emotion: Visuals are a powerful way to evoke emotion, but the audio is even more powerful. Listen to a video meant to elicit strong emotions from the audience with your eyes closed. You can still feel those emotions through the audio. A large part of impactful videos is making your audience feel the emotions you want them to feel. A good example of audio creating emotion is two people having a heated argument. The pitch of their voice and angry words create a tense and angry atmosphere that supports what you want your audience to feel. Emotion is also often conveyed with music.

Saving poor visual quality: Sometimes, audio can even save a video with poor visual quality. Unless perfect visuals are crucial to your video, an audience may be inclined to keep watching because of the value they are getting from the audio.

LET'S TALK ABOUT NOISE

Noise. Sometimes you just can't get away from ambient noise. Noise is literally everywhere unless you're in a sound-proof studio. However, there are some common background noises you can try to work around or make less obvious. Let's look at some indoor and outdoor sounds and how to handle them.

Indoor Noise

The air conditioning unit is one of the most annoying indoor noises that cause video-makers an audio headache. The noise from an air conditioner can range from a slight hum to an audible rumble and even whining if it's not looked after properly. Other noises can filter in from outside the room or building. How do you deal with a humming air conditioner or other sounds when you're trying to shoot a video?

Turn it off: If you have the option, just switch the A/C off while you're shooting.

Cover vents: If you can't control the A/C in a large office building, cover the vents with heavy blankets to dampen the sound being carried through them.

Watch the weather: Sometimes, the weather doesn't play ball, and you risk your subject and crew either freezing their butts off or melting in the heat. If you can't turn the A/C off because of the weather, anticipate the temperatures and prepare the room beforehand. If it's cold out, turn the A/C heat on high and warm the room up as much as is comfortably possible before the shoot. If the weather is sweltering out, turn the A/C chill on full blast to freeze the room (not literally) to cool it down. When you have chilled or heated the room sufficiently, switch the unit off right before you start shooting to shut off the noise but keep the room at a comfortable temperature while you're shooting.

Use blankets: If you are filming in a room where you can hear noise from outside, try covering the windows with heavy blankets to block out some noise.

Ask for quiet: Many YouTubers, and other video-makers, film their videos in their own homes. Now, of course, if you're rooming with someone who isn't the most considerate person, you may run into a brick wall. However, you can ask your room/housemates or spouse for some quiet while you're filming. You need to be considerate of them as well. It's not a good idea to ask the boys to be quiet during a sporting event on TV, and it's not fair to ask someone to tiptoe around the home the entire day.

Outdoor Noise

There isn't all that much you can do about outdoor ambient noise, but you can do a few things to minimize the audio issues.

Pick the quietest location: Scout your locations, listen for ambient noise at the times of day you want to do the filming and pick the quietest location that fits your criteria.

Pick the right microphone: Some microphones are more prone to picking up ambient noise and wind than others. Pick the right mic for the ambient noise in your location.

Position your subject with their back to the wind: if you're using a handheld microphone or one attached to the collar of their clothing, position your subject with their back to the wind. The person's body will offer the mic some shelter from the wind.

Use noise-canceling accessories: There are coverings for microphones that help cancel out some ambient background noises. You have the option of a foam windshield or a wind-jammer (also called a dead cat). Foam windshields are foam coverings that fit over a microphone. If you think about headset mics, they often have a bit of foam around them. These are foam shields to help cancel out background noise.

The same types of coverings are available for larger mics. They are not as effective at blocking out wind and noise as deadcasts, but they will still help dampen noise. If you've ever seen a news crew filming, you have probably seen a fluffy gray covering over the microphone. This is a deadcast. It's a buffer between the wind and the microphone that absorbs the force of the wind to cancel out the sound.

MICROPHONES

Microphones are a vital accessory for making your subject heard in videos. Most cellphone, video camera, DSLR, and mirrorless microphones are not good enough to produce decent audio for a video. They aren't powerful enough to pick up sound from further away, and they pick up too much surrounding sound in general. Your best bet is a separate microphone that plugs into your recording device and allows you to boost your audio recording capabilities.

The first step to picking out a microphone is to know what you're going to be using it for. Are you only going to be filming one type of video or a variety of different 'genres'? You don't just have to consider what you'll be using the microphone for.

You also need to think about the different pickup patterns different microphones have. A pickup pattern is the direction from which your microphone picks up sound. Not all microphones just pick up sound from every direction around them. When you want to record sound, where is it coming from? Is there noise you don't want to record or that you want to minimize from a certain direction? These considerations factor into choosing the right style and pickup pattern for a microphone.

Types of Microphones

There are three main types of microphones. Each mic is designed to perform a specific job. The question is, what job is your microphone going to be doing?

Free-standing: Okay, the name is a little deceiving. Free-standing microphones don't necessarily have to be on a stand; they can easily be handheld microphones. The term 'free-standing' really just separates these microphones from those designed to be attached to a camera, such as shotgun mics. They could be permanently attached to a fixed stand, or they could be detachable and fit into a bracket on a stand. If you think about the microphones you see on stage when an entertainer is performing, that's a free-standing mic. The microphone standing on the desk of someone doing a radio interview or video podcast is also a free-standing mic. Free-standing microphones come in two types:

- Dynamic: These microphones are not as sensitive as condenser mics which means they are positioned closer to the mouth and don't pick up the background noise.
- Condenser: These microphones are more sensitive than dynamic mics, which means they aren't held as

close to the mouth, but they also pick up more background noise.

Shotgun: These microphones have a long, almost conical shape and are usually attached to a camera because they offer directional control for isolating the sound you want to record. These mics are sure to capture sound in the direction you're pointing your camera by attaching one to the camera.

Lavalier: They're also called lapel microphones because they are small and designed to clip onto the neck or lapel of a shirt or t-shirt. These microphones are wireless and help you home in on the person's voice it's attached to. However, lapel mics often have a sound pickup pattern that records audio from every direction. This means you need to ensure good visuals because the audio may not always be that great.

Pickup Patterns

There are six essential pickup patterns you need to know about before choosing a microphone.

Omnidirectional: Mics with this pickup pattern up pick up sound from every direction, in front, behind, on either side, below, above, and everything in between. This is the most versatile pickup pattern, but it also records the most background or ambient noise. Omnidirectional mics are good for recording sound from a moving subject or during an interview. Many lavaliers or lapel mics are omnidirectional.

Bidirectional: Picks up sound equally well in front of and behind the microphone. These are good for radio interviews and recording video podcasts but not much else.

Unidirectional: These are also called lobar microphones, and they focus their pickup pattern mainly on the front. This unforgiving pickup pattern doesn't pick up much sound from either side or behind the mic. If you work with moving subjects or cannot have the microphone pointed directly at the subject, it's probably not a great choice. Usually, a unidirectional pickup pattern is found in shotgun microphones but other types of mics can have this pattern.

Cardioid: This pickup pattern is a great 'all-rounder'. It's flexible and forgiving but also a tad noisy. The sound is gathered in front of the microphone and the sides to an extent. Most of the sound from behind the mic isn't picked up. It's a good choice for events, weddings, and documentaries.

Hyper-cardioid: This is a typical shotgun mic pickup pattern that offers you the directionality to home in on the sound in front of the microphone while minimizing sound from either side and behind the microphone. The mic is more directional than the cardioid but not as directional as the super-cardioid. These are great for documentaries.

Super-cardioid: These microphones can isolate the sound in front of them more than the hyper-cardioid pickup pattern but aren't as strict as the unidirectional lobar pattern. You will have more margin for error if there is a slight movement while recording without losing the audio you're trying to focus on. The super-cardioid pattern is only found in shotgun mics used on-camera or on a boom pole.

MUSIC

Music is a powerful video tool because it helps set the tone for a scene or create a mood. It's something you should definitely consider using in your video, but how do you go about deciding when and where to use music and what style to choose?

Setting the tone: The style of music you choose will partly be decided by the mood or tone of your video. You're not going to use upbeat music in a scene or video that's meant to be gloomy and vice versa. There are exceptions when you can break the rule for artistic impact, such as syncing an action sequence to a piece of classical music. However, you should generally match the energy and mood of the music to the tone of the footage.

How much music should you use? Not all videos require music to play throughout the entire video. That's not to say you should ditch it completely. Various types of video can benefit from using music as 'bookends' on either side of the video. You can use music as part of the introduction and conclusion of the video, with no music in between. Using music to introduce the video can quickly and easily set the tone for the video to follow, setting up the viewer's expectation of what's about to happen. It's a good idea to use the same music for the intro and the 'outro' instead of using different pieces of music. It helps keep continuity and links the end of the video back to the beginning.

Vocal or instrumental? Music with vocals can be very distracting if you're laying it over a video that has dialogue. Your audience might find themselves listening to the song's lyrics and not to the person speaking. The only time it's safe to use music with vocals is during a scene where there are no dialogue subtitles/captions. For everything else, stick with instrumental music to be on the safe side.

Forget duration: Songs have a duration from beginning to end, but that doesn't mean you need to fill the whole song duration with video footage. Short, punchy videos lose their impact when they run on longer than they really should, even if it's just a minute. Cut the music, loop it, and stitch it together to compliment your video. Don't fall victim to the duration trap by filling the music with video instead of matching music to your video.

Beware of synthetic music: Music can easily be synthesized digitally instead of using real instruments to create a song. Beware of using MIDI music as it can sound unprofessional and cheap, which will bring the quality of your video down by association. Wherever possible, always choose music produced using real instruments.

Important note: Be aware of digital rights management (DRM). It's a system used to protect the rights of digital work copyright holders. When a video is made for public consumption, always be cautious to read the "fine print" and ensure you have a legal right/permission to use the work or source your music from DRM-free sources.

BOTTOM LINE

Now that you have all the knowledge you need to start filming, it's time to get into the steps of the actual filming itself. You need to consider various aspects while filming, and we're about to cover that in the next part of this book. You should read the entire next part of the book before you even decide to start filming. The intricacies of filming may lead you back to the planning stage to tweak some of your ideas in order to refine and clarify them before you set foot on set.

Let's look at what you need to know about filming your video in the next part, which focuses on the filming process.

SHARING THE KNOWLEDGE

"Filmmaking is the ultimate team sport."

–Michael Keaton

As your skills improve and you learn more about what makes a good video, you're probably starting to notice the flaws in more of the content you watch online.

Perhaps you're even frustrated about how poor-quality video gets in the way of your ability to enjoy the narrative or learn from the information presented.

This frustration is a valuable part of your learning experience... but it may not be helping you to enjoy everything you watch online.

But you have an opportunity to reach out and help some of those other video creators step up their game... and all it takes is a few moments of your time.

Helping other creators improve doesn't threaten your success as a video producer... A little competition will only strengthen your resolve and motivate you to improve even more... So why not help other creators to rise with you?

By leaving a review of this book on Amazon, you'll show other video makers where they can find all the information they need to improve their skills.

And the more people do that, the better the quality of the content across your screen will be. Simply by letting other readers know how this book has helped you and what they'll find inside it, you'll show them that there's no shame in having more to learn… and they'll discover exactly what they can do to take their content to the next level.

Thank you for your support. Our mission is to help as many people as possible learn the skills required to make high-quality professional videos… and the more people do that, the better the experience for everyone.

Please visit the link below or scan the QR code to leave feed-back on Amazon.

https://www.amazon.com/review/create-review/?
asin=1739816285

PART IV

SHOOTING YOUR VIDEO

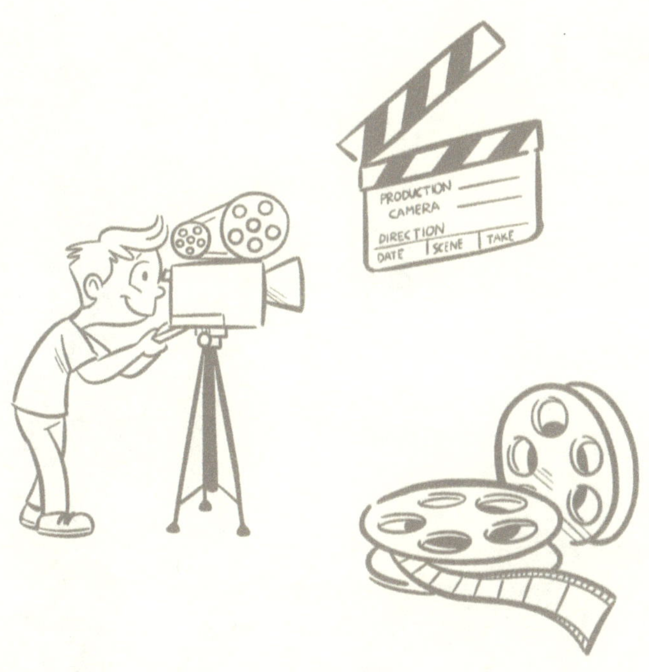

12

IT'S ALL ABOUT THE SHOT

All visual representations of literally anything are about the shot. Whether you are shooting stills photography, creating a sketch, or filming a video, the shot you capture will define what you are trying to convey. There are literally dozens and dozens of different types of shots you can choose from, but we're going to focus on the most essential shots for improving the quality of your video.

TYPES OF SHOTS

There are three basic categories the different shots can be divided into. They are the size and angle of a shot and the movement of the camera. Each category has several shots that fall under them. Often, all three categories can be found in a single shot as you combine the size, angle, and camera movement to create the shot.

Size of the Shot

The size of the shot indicates the size of the subject relative to the frame of your shot. Does your subject appear as a small dot in the distance with lots of surrounding landscape? Does your subject dominate the frame, taking up so much space that little else can be seen around it? You need to know a few essential shot sizes to start improving your video right now.

The Close-Up (CU)

Close-up shots are a common type used in both video and photography. The idea is to fill the shot with your subject so that little else is visible around them. This type of shot focuses on the subject by removing as much potential surrounding distraction as possible. Another reason the subject commands focus in a close-up shot is that the bigger something is, in comparison to what's around it, the more visible it is, and the more your eye will be drawn to it.

There are a few variations of the close-up shot:

- Extreme close-up: Typically, only the subject's eyes are visible, or, if your subject is an object, perhaps only a piece of patterning or text is visible and not the whole object.
- Close-up: The subject's face dominates the frame from forehead to chin.
- Medium close-up: The subject is visible from the chest up.

Medium Shot (MS)

The medium shot lies between the standard close-up and a long shot. In these shots, the subject is visible from head to waist height. Unlike the close-up, where only facial expression is visible, the medium shot allows viewers to see some of the subject's body language as well.

Long Shot (LS)

The long-shot is on the other end of the spectrum from the close-up shot. In a long shot, the subject's size compared to the surroundings is visible. It might show a landscape with the subject barely visible (often called an extreme-long shot) until the subject starts dominating the frame from head to feet (also called a full shot). Long shots serve two purposes. They give the audience a sense of where the filming is taking place, adding to the context and meaning of the video. They can also be used to distance the audience, separating them as onlookers instead of making them feel part of the action.

The Angle of the Shot

Shot angles are another consideration when planning your shots. You already have one aspect of perspective when you choose your shot size. Now it's time to make that perspective even more dynamic by picking the angle. What does angle offer you that shot size doesn't? The camera angle can help you create atmosphere and emotion in your viewers by changing their perspective of the scene.

Eye-Level

The name pretty much gives this angle away. An eye-level camera allows viewers to connect with the subject because we normally look at other people at eye level. There is no sense of being looked down on or looking down on the subject. Eye-level puts the viewer on the same level as the subject, creating neutrality and a sense of connection between them.

Tip: Eye-level doesn't mean you have to be shooting a close-up of the subject's face. You can achieve an eye-level angle from a distance; it simply means that the camera is neither pointed up nor down on the subject.

High Angles

High angles refer to those angles where the camera looks down on the subject and can range from slightly higher to much higher. Two things you can achieve with a high angle are making the subject appear smaller or making them seem subordinate. At the same time, the viewer feels bigger or superior (especially if the camera is acting as the 'eyes' of another character.

An extreme high angle from very far up is called a 'bird's-eye view' because the camera takes a perspective similar to that of a bird flying over the scene.

Low Angles

As you can probably guess, low angles are shot from lower than the subject as if looking up at them. Low angles have the opposite effects of a high angle. They make the subject appear bigger while the viewer feels smaller, and they also can make the subject seem superior or intimidating while the viewer feels subordinate or threatened,

A worm's-eye view is a type of low-angled shot that looks up at a subject in a way that makes them seem enormous and gives the viewer a sense of being as small and low to the ground as a worm.

Point-of-View (POV)

For the point-of-view shot, the camera shows the viewer the scene from the subject's perspective. If you were to hold a camera up to your eye and start filming, everything you are recording is from your point of view. Point-of-view shots are useful for making the audience feel like they are a part of the scene and evoke emotion. When the camera angle shows you what you would see if you were the one actually there watching it, you're more likely to feel engaged. The sense of separation from the scene diminishes.

Over-the-Shoulder (OTS)

Over-the-shoulder shots place a character in front of the camera with their back to it. The camera is "looking over their shoulder". This angle is used to show characters in a discussion, during a confrontation, or to give you a different perspective of what the character sees when looking out over a landscape or other scene. It's an alternative take on the classic point-of-view shot.

Dutch Angle

Most camera angles use horizontal and/or vertical lines, such as a horizon, to show that the shot is straight. The Dutch angle purposefully skews the angle to create distortion, which then creates a sense of disorientation and unease in the viewer. You only need to tilt the camera to one side, so it's not being held level. For example, most shots would frame a person perfectly upright, but you would tilt the camera with a Dutch angle, so the person is skewed. The degree of 'skewness' is up to you and what you are trying to achieve.

Camera Movement

Along with the size and angle of the shot, you can create even more dynamic video by including camera movement. There are two key ways to do this.

Zoom

You can zoom either by physically moving the camera closer to or further away from your subject or by using the camera's zoom function. Zooming in can draw the audience's attention to a specific part of the scene or to the subject's face to emphasize facial expression and emotion. On the other hand, zooming out can reveal the "bigger picture".

Tip 1: Unless you're aiming for an artsy appeal or shocking movement, zooming should be done with consistency at a slow to moderate speed.

Tip 2: Wherever possible, opt to zoom in or out by walking instead of using a zoom lens. Many things can go wrong using a zoom lens. People could step into your shot because you're too far away for them to notice you're filming. You could lose audio quality by being too far away from the speaker. However, if you are going to zoom by physically moving the camera, you may want to invest in a gimbal to help reduce the movement shake that naturally happens as you walk.

Tilt or Pan

Panning and tilting are the simplest movements you can make with a camera. Take a moment to think of your head as a camera. Tilting would be lowering or lifting your head to look up or down. Panning would be moving your head from side to side to look around you.

While tilting could be misconstrued as an angle, it's not the same thing. Tilting refers to the movement the camera is making, which is being caught on film. Let's go back to imagining your head as a camera, and you're sitting opposite a friend. You would start out looking at the person at eye level, and if they were to stand up, you would tilt your head with their movement to transition to looking at them from a low angle.

Tip 1: Hand holding to tilt and pan can introduce a lot of camera shake and create skew shots. For the best results, mount your camera on a tripod with a tilt/pan head. The tripod offers stability and keeps the shot straight while allowing fluid movement.

Tip 2: Tilt and pan speed can vary greatly from slow to so quick that things become a blur. Different scenes may call for different speeds. For instance, slow panning or tilting can indicate trepidation and caution, while fast panning can indicate sudden action or that a subject is moving at high speed. Play around with tilt or pan speed to find what works for your scene.

Other Types of Shots

Establishing Shot

This shot sets the scene by showing your viewers where your subject is so viewers can orient themselves within the scene. Establishing shots are often wide and provide contextual cues such as buildings and landmarks or elements inside the room that give the audience an idea of what room they are in. The establishing shot should be used whenever your video transitions to a new scene, not only at the beginning of the video.

Single, Two, or Three Shot

A single, two- or three-shot doesn't refer to the size or angle of the frame or movement of the camera. Instead, you're just categorizing the shot by how many subjects are in it.

BOTTOM LINE

There's more to filming than just pointing a camera at your subject. The shot angle, size, and camera movement can be used to give your video more meaning by conveying subliminal messages and even emotion. However, that's not all there is to framing your shot for maximum effect. In the next chapter, we look at composition rules that will help you structure a more effective shot.

COMPOSING THE SHOT

The composition of a shot is how the visual elements of a shot are positioned to make that shot pleasing to the eye and convey the information you want to share. Most of the basic composition rules are subtle, but they profoundly affect the quality of your video.

RULE OF THIRDS

If you divide your shot by drawing two horizontal and two vertical lines through it, all evenly spaced, you will end up with a nine-block grid. The rule of thirds is composing your shot so that critical visual elements are placed along those grid lines. It is especially effective when those elements are arranged in the areas where the four lines intersect.

Now, you may think that humans automatically want to see a scene that is more-or-less symmetrical with the subject placed smack-dab in the center. While balance and symmetry have a time and a place, most of the time, an off-center arrangement just looks better.

The grid lines and intersections can be used to position important elements in a shot, such as:

- Mountain peaks
- Horizons
- Tall buildings and trees
- Prominent pieces of furniture
- Human and animal subjects
- Anything you want to draw attention to

Tip: Using the rule of thirds takes practice. Sometimes it works, and sometimes it doesn't. Sometimes you need to shift your key elements slightly off the grid lines. There will be instances where a subtler off-center orientation looks better than a more obvious one. While you're getting the hang of the rule of thirds, experiment with shifting elements around to find the most pleasing arrangement to the eye.

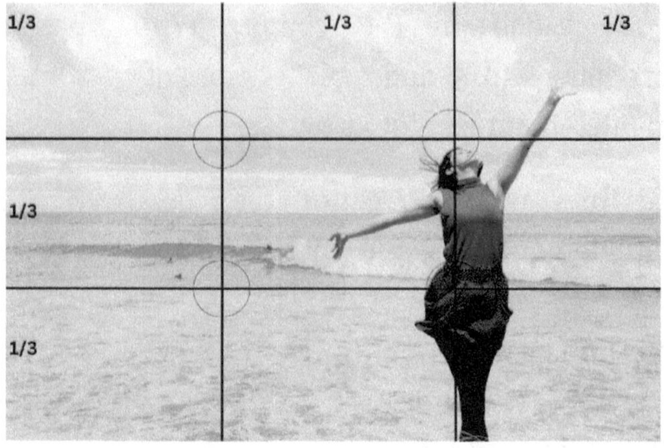

Breaking the Rule of Thirds

Breaking the rule of thirds means creating balance and symmetry in your shot. There are many times the rule works, but there are also times when it doesn't. However, knowing when and how to break the rule takes practice. There are three ways to break the rule.

Center

The most obvious way to break the rule of thirds is by placing the subject or prominent elements horizontally or vertically dead center in your shot. Centering a subject can draw your viewers' focus to the subject and direct their attention away from the 'stage' or background. It's especially effective if your shot is oriented in portrait (upright as opposed to lengthwise in landscape) or square.

Tip: When placing your crucial element in the center, make sure it is precisely dead center, horizontally or vertically.

Your composition won't be as effective if it's even slightly off-center.

Extreme Edges

Almost the opposite of centering, using the extreme edges of your frame can be visually powerful. To use the extremes, place your key element close to the edge of your shot. Unlike centering, using the very edges of your frame is not hugely popular because it only works in a handful of circumstances and requires both skill and a keen eye.

Tip: Be cautious of placing your key element too close to the edge of your frame. It should have enough 'breathing room' away from the edge, or you risk losing the effect and end up with a shot that looks like you just have no eye for composition whatsoever.

Cornering

Most of the time, we are so focussed on either side or top and bottom of a shot that we forget it has corners that can also be utilized. Similarly to using the extreme edges of your frame, using the corners only works in a handful of cases. It requires skill to pull off, but it can give your shot the 'wow' factor when it works.

THE 180-DEGREE RULE

This rule is pretty simple. Whenever you have two main characters in a scene, they should stay in the same order they first appear in, from left to right. You shouldn't cut to a camera angle from the opposite side where the character initially on the left is now on the right, and the one on the right is on the left.

If you are filming moving objects, the 180-degree rule also applies but in a slightly different way. If you are filming something moving from right to left, don't switch angles to the other side and film it from left to right while still going in the same direction. It will look like the object turned around and is heading back the way it came.

Breaking this compositional rule can be disorienting for your audience and make your video confusing and awkward.

Tip 1: If you need to or want to use different camera angles within the 180-degree rule, draw a straight line parallel to the characters in the shot and only use camera angles along that line.

Tip 2: If you want to change camera angles to the opposite side of the characters, show the camera's movement in the shot. This means moving the camera from one side of the subject to the other while filming. This shows the audience the character being 'flipped' to the opposite side of the shot so viewers can stay oriented.

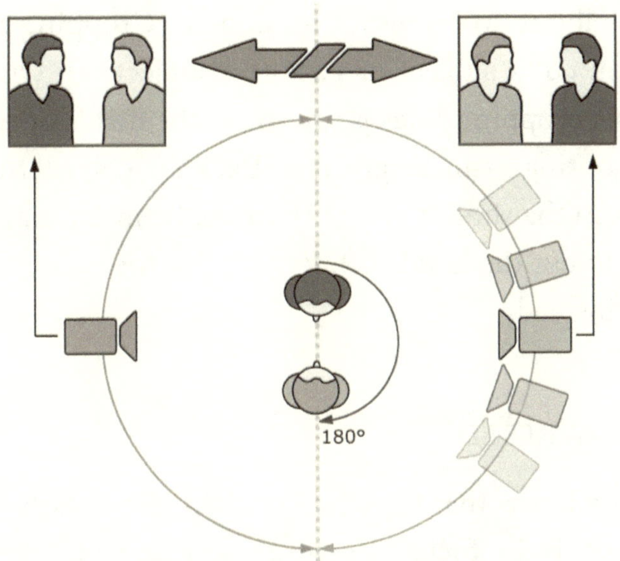

HEADROOM AND CROPPING

Headroom is the space between the top of the frame and the top of the subject's head. The rule of thirds for headroom doesn't apply in close-up and medium close-up shots. Leaving a third of the frame open between the top of a subject's head and the top of the frame (unless there is a significantly important element high above the subject) doesn't look good. You have all this 'empty' space that isn't doing anything for your video. On the other hand, leaving too little space or, even worse, cutting off a bit of the top of a subject's head also ruins the shot and looks awkward.

Tip: If you look at the rule of thirds above, an average headroom would be a third to half of the top third of the frame between the top of the subject's head and the top.

Let's talk about cropping for a moment. Cropping refers to where you cut a subject or part of a subject off. One of the most basic cropping rules is not to cut the hands or feet off if you're shooting a full-length shot. Back up a bit till the whole subject is in the shot. If you're shooting from the waist up, be sure not to cut the hands off. Rather, opt for a shot from the chest up instead.

DEPTH OF FIELD

We already know that the depth of field affects how much of your scene is in focus. However, unless you are using a DSLR, mirrorless, or professional video camera, you may not be able to adjust the aperture to change the depth of field. If you can't press a button or turn a dial to make the change, you're going to have to move your subject. Depth of field is relative to the distance of your subject from the camera and the distance between your subject and the background.

For a shallower depth of field: move your subject closer to the camera and further away from the background to blur the background.

For a wider depth of field: move your subject further from the camera and closer to the background to keep the background more in focus.

Tip: If your background isn't essential, blurring it can hide imperfections and minimize distractions for viewers. A blurry background with an in-focus subject directs the audience's entire focus to that subject.

FOCUS ON THE IMPORTANT DETAILS

When composing your shot, it's important to understand the power of paying attention to the details and choosing the right hero or main subject. Details have a powerful influence on the appearance of a scene and how the viewer perceives and interprets the message being sent. Likewise, focusing on the correct subject will help you convey what you really want to say without it getting "lost in translation".

Picking the Right Hero

You may think your main character will be the focus in a scene with two people, but that isn't always the case. Depending on what you want to tell the audience, your focus will change even if your scene doesn't. It's all about the camera angle and what you choose to highlight in the shot.

Let's look at how picking the right hero can change the message being sent to the audience.

Picture this: an employee and a boss are seated at a desk. To decide what you need to focus on, go back to your script and focus on the description of the shot. Let's imagine three possible scenarios:

1. The boss gives the employee a poor performance evaluation. In this shot, you would focus on the boss

and what he has to say about the employee's performance.

2. The employee is refused a raise. Focusing on the employee would highlight him stating his case for receiving a raise. You can show the disappointment on his face when he's told 'no' because his performance isn't up to scratch.

3. The employee gets fired. Turning the focus to the boss's hand resting on a notice of termination in his desk drawer tells the audience that the employee is beyond redemption and will get fired.

Can you see how the same scene can have different heroes depending on the message you want to send to your audience?

Same Hero + Different Details = Different Message

Composing your scene according to your message is as important as picking the right hero.

Picture this: a woman is purchasing a pair of ballet shoes, and the hero of the shot is her taking money out of her purse while the ballet shoes are visible on the counter. The details of that shot will tell a different story despite the hero being the same for different stories. Here are two scenarios:

1. A woman is whipping a gold credit card out of a high-end purse with plenty of crisp high-value notes as we see shiny new ballet shoes in the background. These visual cues tell the audience she's wealthy.

Your viewers may even perceive that the ballet shoes are just something she's purchasing for her daughter because she does ballet as a hobby and needs a new pair.

2. A woman is opening a tatty purse with only a few grubby low-value notes in it as we see visibly worn, second-hand ballet shoes in the background. So, the audience knows that she's not wealthy. Your viewers could perceive that the woman can't really afford it. Therefore, whatever the reason, buying the shoes is incredibly important to her. Perhaps her daughter is an aspiring dancer who has been given a scholarship to a prestigious dance school, but her family is too poor to afford new shoes. However, having her daughter follow her dreams is so important to the mother that she's doing everything to support her.

On the flip side, not using details to emphasize your message could mean your audience doesn't have a true grasp of the message you want to send. Let's take a look at how a lack of attention to detail can detract from the importance of the message in the second example above.

The woman has the kind of purse an average woman would own. There is an average amount of cash inside that's neither crisp nor grubby. The ballet shoes in the background look pretty average too. Your message of the struggle to support her daughter following her dreams is lost.

BOTTOM LINE

Following some basic composition rules helps make your video look more professional and drives home the information you're trying to provide to your audience. Once you understand these rules, you can start employing other techniques to improve how you actually film the video, which we'll cover in the next chapter.

14

HOW TO IMPROVE FILMING A VIDEO

Once you grasp composition rules and how to employ them to improve the quality of your scene setup, it's time to start filming. You can use some techniques to enhance your video quality while filming, and we're about to get into those techniques.

CHOOSE THE RIGHT FRAME RATE

The frame rate impacts how smooth your footage looks, but that doesn't necessarily mean a higher frame rate is automatically better. Here are some tips for deciding on the correct frame rate:

- A higher frame rate keeps fast-paced motion smooth and the details in your video sharp.

- Faster frame rates capture less motion blur, keeping a moving object in sharp focus. This can appear unnatural to the human eye because our eyes naturally observe some motion blur when looking at high-speed objects.
- Choosing a frame rate that's too slow for fast-moving objects can result in a choppy appearance.
- Using slow motion calls for a higher frame rate to keep the video smooth when playback is slowed down.
- Higher frame rates mean bigger file sizes.
- 24fps is considered the minimum speed to shoot at, because the human eye starts to see smooth motion, as opposed to choppy frames, at 24fps. Busy scenes will show a lot of motion blur at this speed.
- 30fps has become the standard speed for shooting TV footage. It's suitable for scenes capturing a lot of motion.
- 60+fps is used for capturing slow-slow motion footage and extremely high-speed moving subjects.

SHOOT SHORT SHOTS

Less is sometimes more, and video-making is the perfect example. Long shots can become boring, and your audience may lose focus. Shooting shorter shots is the way to go to keep your audience engaged. Now, shooting short shots doesn't mean you should keep the scenes short. You need to keep different shots short, regardless of the length of the scene. Cutting to different angles makes your audience think. Seeing different angles, even of the same scene, makes our brains work to figure out what's going on and perceive meaning from each shot.

Cutting to different angles can also help you convey more information by showing your viewers different details. However, always bear the 180-degree rule in mind, so your shots flow, and your scene doesn't get flipped 180 degrees unless you move the camera while filming to show that transition.

How long should your shots be? There is no solid rule about shot length, but a rule of thumb many filmmakers follow is no more than 20 seconds. By 30 seconds, your audience has gotten used to the scene; they've taken in most of it and derived meaning from it. Any longer than that, and their brain says, "Okay, I've seen this. What's next?".

Tip: Consider each shot and what you want to tell your audience. Sometimes a longer shot is necessary to provide all the information you need to get across. In this case, viewers will be absorbing information throughout and aren't likely to get bored.

MAKE LONG DIALOGUE SCENES MORE INTERESTING

Let's face it, long dialogue scenes can quickly become a snore-fest. We know we just told you to keep shots short, but how do you keep a long dialogue scene visually interesting?

We will give you a few techniques to shake things up, but before we can do that, let's look at an example of a scene where a long dialogue may be necessary.

The scene: Bank robbers discuss their plans to pull off a bank heist. The dialogue involves the bank's security, time scales, past mistakes robbing banks, characters coming up with ideas, and back and forth arguing.

Move Characters

If you have more than two characters, have one of them leave the scene to fetch something and reappear with whatever they went to get. All the while, the other characters keep the dialogue going.

Move the Camera

Moving the camera can be done in several ways.

- Cut from a wide shot to close-ups of the different characters. To avoid this simple cut getting boring, use different close-up shots like extreme and medium shots to convey different characters' emotion and body language while speaking.
- Move the camera around the scene without cutting to show the audience the movement, such as circling a table they may be sitting at.
- Have a character leave the scene and follow that character to a different location. Keep the moving character engaged in the dialogue with the others

while moving. Alternatively, keep the dialogue in the other location audible.

- Have a character leave the scene while you're still focused on those in the scene. Have the moving character keep up the dialogue and cut to a close-up of the character when they talk, such as when they are asked a question or when they're saying something that creates tension.

When to Move the Camera

We've told you to shoot short shots, but that's not to say you should move the camera purely to keep the shot short. Moving the camera should be done with purpose. Otherwise, you're filling your video with random shots, making you look like you don't know what you're doing. Your audience will be wondering, "Why are we moving?" as they search for the significance of the new shot. If there is no significance, they'll get bored, annoyed, and their mind will wander. Another reason viewers could get frustrated with random camera movement is if something interesting is happening, but they don't have time to process what's happening, or they wanted to see more, but you moved away to a shot that makes no sense. They'll feel cheated out of what they perceive as valuable visual information.

Before moving the camera, ask yourself:

- Why am I moving? What's the motivation?

- What shot will I cut to that gives the viewer more information the previous shot wasn't providing?

WHEN ENOUGH IS ENOUGH

There are a few reasons you could get carried away and shoot far too much video footage:

1. You're having a lot of fun because filming is the most exciting part of making a video.
2. You're not confident in your video-making abilities. You are afraid you won't have the right shot, or the shot may be inadequately filmed. So, you do it repeatedly just in case.
3. You come up with loads of new ideas for shots while you're filming, and you want to capture them all.

You will have to learn when to say, "That's a wrap."

- Keep in mind your timeframe and costs to avoid getting too caught up in the fun of filming.
- Develop your confidence as a video maker to avoid re-shooting shots when there isn't really anything wrong with the first take.
- Keep an open mind toward new ideas that pop up while filming. However, unless you come up with something absolutely awesome, try to stick with your original plan.

If you aren't careful, the ramifications of shooting too much footage could include:

- Going over your time 'budget'.
- Incurring additional costs you can't afford
- Owing extra favors to people helping you out
- Spending a ton more time editing
- Making decisions on what to keep in the video and what to leave out more difficult

HANDHOLDING TIPS

You might not always have a tripod handy, or it may just not be practical to use one because you're going to be moving your camera around. Here are some tips to stabilize your handheld camera to minimize movement shake:

- **Use both hands:** They say, "Two heads are better than one." When filming, two hands are more stable than one.
- **Hold the camera close to your body:** The further away you hold the camera, the more your arms will shake, especially when the muscles get tired.
- **Use simple camera movements:** The more you move the camera and the more complicated or challenging moving the camera into the position is, the more shake you're likely to get.
- **Visualize a cup of water:** Think of your camera as a cup filled with water. You're more likely to keep your

knees bent and your shoulders more relaxed to counteract the up and down movement that naturally happens while walking.

- **Pan in an arc; don't pivot:** Shuffling your feet to pivot your whole body while panning creates shake. Rotate from your waist while keeping your feet in place for a 180-degree pan. For a 360-degree pan, try using a swivel chair if you can.
- **Lean against a wall to create a human tripod:** Nobody can stand absolutely perfectly still. Your body naturally moves, even when you're standing in place. Brace your back against a wall with your feet spread about shoulder-width apart to minimize that movement.

RAINY WEATHER TIPS

- **Avoid filming in the rain:** Water and camera equipment don't play well together. Avoid shooting in the rain unless you have no choice.
- **Use silica gel in your camera bag:** You should always choose a camera bag with a protective rain cover, but a cover isn't a guarantee no moisture will reach your bag. Stash a bag of silica gel in your camera bag. It will help absorb moisture.
- **Use a rain cover:** Professional rain covers may not be cheap, but they are worth the investment if you can afford them. Their quality ensures the best possible protection from rain and splashes.

- **Don't use your clothes:** Clothes aren't really clean once you put them on. Skin oils and other dirt particles start gathering on the fabric almost immediately, which will leave smudges and marks. If you have a lot of water on your lens, you can dab it (don't wipe as some materials are rough) with your clothes and then use a microfiber cloth to dry it completely.
- **Use lens covers for DSLR and mirrorless cameras:** The lenses available for these cameras can be fitted with a plastic cover called a lens hood. Lens hoods will help minimize water droplets on your lens.
- **Dry your gear:** Take the time to use absorbent cloths or towels to wipe down your camera equipment as soon as possible after being exposed to moisture.
- **Opt for battery-operated lights:** Electricity and water aren't good bedfellows. Battery-operated lights take mains electricity out of the equation.

BONUS TIP: Make an improvised rain cover.

1. Put your camera inside a plastic bag.
2. Cut a hole out of the bag for the lens to poke through. Make sure the hole is just big enough to fit the lens through and only just allow the very tip of the lens to stick out.
3. Use gaffer tape to tape the plastic bag around the lens to stop it from shifting further up the lens, exposing more of it, or the hole from widening.

4. Pull the other end of the plastic bag over the camera and your hands to shield it from the rain while still being able to use it.

5. You can also do the same using a trash bag and pulling the whole trash bag over your head to keep your head and shoulders dry.

WHAT NOT TO FORGET BEFORE PRESSING RECORD

Sometimes it's easy to overlook a few crucial things before pressing that record button. Even if you're convinced you did it when prepping your camera gear the day before, here's what to double-check:

- **File type:** File format affects two aspects of your raw video footage; the file size and the video quality. The larger, uncompressed file formats yield the best quality video, but the files will take up more memory.
- **Lens:** A dirty lens will result in blurred sections of your frame or unsightly spots even if it just has specks on it. Ensure your lens is clean and free from specks and smudges.
- **Format cards**: Memory cards need to be formatted to ensure the camera reads the card properly. It also prevents you from mixing old footage from a previous shoot with the new recordings.

Tip 1: Format your memory card every time you use a new card, not just the first one you pop in to start recording with.

Tip 2: Check your file format when replacing the memory card or battery. Most cameras will remember the settings, but sometimes they don't.

BOTTOM LINE

No matter how well you prepare to shoot your video, it will not look professional if you don't film it well. These tips and techniques for choosing the right frame rate, moving the camera, and how to shoot in various situations will refine your filming skill and knowledge. It will help you create better quality videos that people will want to watch.

Not all video projects can be shot in the same way or use the same planning tips. In the next chapter, we'll explore a couple of common video projects that need special attention to aspects that will help your video hit its mark.

15

TIPS FOR SHOOTING SPECIFIC PROJECTS

Different video projects have different needs that need to be met to improve the quality and make them look more professional. Let's look at a few common video projects and how to film them better.

INTERVIEWS

Choose the right person for the job: Opt for interesting people who aren't camera shy and have the knowledge you're looking for. Here are some other tips to help interviews go smoothly:

- **Prepare your questions beforehand:** It doesn't matter if you're interviewing someone you know or a stranger. Know who you're interviewing and what you're going to ask.

- **Make interviewees comfortable:** Video will show the audience the interviewee's body language. Get them to relax, use their hands while talking, and tell them not to worry too much about what they say because you can cut bits out.
- **Allow the interviewee to set the pace:** Don't rush slow talkers or throw too many questions at them. Pick up the pace for fast speakers to prevent them from getting impatient.
- **Look at each other, not the camera:** Staring into the camera makes you and the interviewee look disconnected and create awkwardness, which will show in the video.
- **Have a real conversation:** Pay attention to each other and focus on what is said and asked. Paying attention allows you to pick up on interesting information you could delve deeper into and, in turn, could make the interview more dynamic, informative, and entertaining. People love listening to conversations, not a questions and answers session.
- **Use an appropriate location:** Make it relevant to the interview topic and interviewee and avoid blank backgrounds.
- **Audio is key:** Interviews are all about what's being said, so quality audio is a must.

COLLEGE/JOB APPLICATIONS

- **Don't recite your resume, application essay, or cover letter:** You're sending that in already, and nobody wants to waste time watching you ramble off what they've already read about you.
- **Make it different:** You've already provided a rundown of your qualifications, skills, and work and educational history. Your video is your opportunity to do something different. You could interview a role model, showcase relevant talent, put together a video about something you're passionate about, or document a research project. These are just a few examples. Think outside of the box.
- **If you're camera-shy, don't face the camera:** You don't have to be the star of your video to be in it or have it be about you. For instance, you could narrate it as a voice-over or interview past teachers, employers, or friends about how they view you, like a video reference.
- **Add some humor:** This is only applicable if you can pull off naturally being funny. If not, stiff, awkward, and lame jokes won't hit the mark. When done right, your video becomes entertaining and immediately grabs more attention than a boring recital of a resume.

Bonus Tip: Read Chapter Three again and really think about whether your application should be a video or whether it would be showcased better in another medium.

INSTRUCTIONAL VIDEOS

- **Learn to speak in a teaching voice:** A good teaching voice uses tone and inflection to hold attention and come across as understanding and patient, not self-important or condescending.
- **Pick one point to explain:** As tempting as it is to explain more than one thing, if you are really keen to share your knowledge, don't. People usually want to watch a short video that explains what they want to know now and nothing else.
- **Don't ramble:** Keep it concise. Nobody wants to watch you dawdle or listen to unnecessary waffle. Will your video be effective if you don't say something you're thinking of adding in? If so, leave it out.
- **Ditch the jargon:** Not everybody knows the 'lingo' that experts on a topic use. If it's a video for beginners, keep it simple and plainly stated.
- **Make the steps clear:** Don't rush through a demonstration or leave out explanations or demonstrations of every step.

PRODUCTS AND SERVICES

- **Serve a need:** Potential customers watch a product or service advertisement because they need your product. Sell your wares based on actual needs, not just because it's a great product or service. For example, selling a food delivery service may identify the need for food, the lack of time to make it, the convenience you offer, and the satisfaction you deliver.

- **Create a relationship with viewers:** You want to make your potential customers feel understood. Show them you understand the pain, struggle, or unhappiness that comes from their unmet need in order to spark a feeling of connection with you or your company.

- **Entertain:** If it's not entertaining from the get-go, potential customers will click away before you can pitch your product or service. If it's not entertaining all the way through, they won't stick around to build that relationship that will make them want to buy.

BOTTOM LINE

Every single video needs to be treated as an individual as unique as each different person. They will all present their own challenges and require different techniques and planning. However, some tips still apply to certain types of videos across the board. Combining these tips with each project's individual attention will create a more effective video.

You still have one more step after you've finished shooting your video before you can start getting it out there. We look at post-production in the next part to help you round off your video the right way.

PART V

POST PRODUCTION

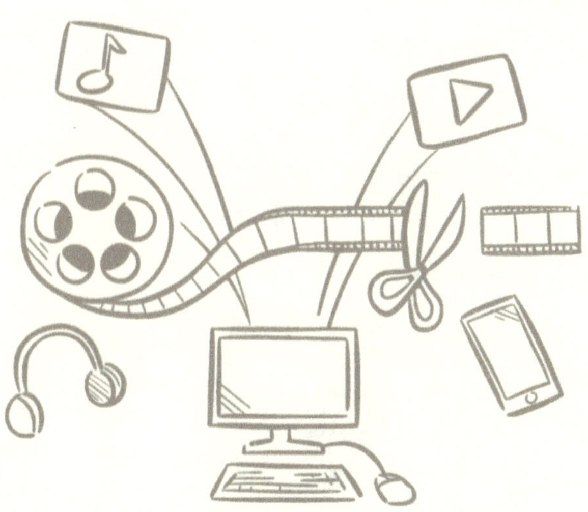

16

EDITING YOUR VIDEO

Good editing is just as crucial as shooting good footage. Actually, editing can be more important than perfect shooting because you can correct some mistakes and improve video quality to a certain extent during post-processing.

BE RUTHLESS

Editing can be hard. Your video is your baby. You've brought it all the way through planning, setting up, and filming, but now it's time to become a cold-blooded killer. You're going to go through your footage, dissect it, and cut out a lot of it. What should you be cutting, and what should you be keeping?

- **Delete bad takes:** Find the best one and delete the rest if you have multiple takes of the same shot.
- **Trim shots down:** Cut out the mediocre, boring, or downright awful parts of shots. Even if it's not horrible, cut it out if it's not great.
- **Say bye-bye to unhelpful footage:** Dump it if it doesn't support your story. Even if it's good, it goes if it's not useful. For instance, if you shot an interview and it went off-topic, no matter how great that anecdote, joke, or comment was, it doesn't have anything to do with your topic and gets cut.

RELATE SEQUENTIAL SHOTS

Your video is telling a story. Sequential shots in a single scene must relate to each other; otherwise, your story becomes a guessing game for the audience, leading to boredom. Each shot that follows another must continue the story you're telling in the scene and keep adding information until the viewer gets the whole story.

Good example: The first shot shows a little girl picking flowers in front of her house. Cut to the little girl walking into the house through the front door. Cut to the little girl giving her mother the flowers.

This example tells a story. Each shot is related to the one before and leads into the next, and the story of a little girl picking flowers for her mother is told.

Bad example: The first shot shows a little girl picking

flowers in front of her house. Cut to the little girl kicking a ball. Cut to the little girl getting into the car with her mother and driving off.

This example doesn't tell a story. The shots are disjointed, and they don't give the audience any real information or message.

EDIT SEAMLESSLY

A scene comprises various shots 'stitched' together to make up that scene. You want each shot to transition into the next without a noticeable 'jump'. A jump is when the movement or dialogue from one shot doesn't match up with the next. The video appears to 'jump'.

Good example 1: A woman is drinking a cup of tea. The first shot shows the tea being poured from the teapot. The next shot shows her raising the cup to her lips and taking a sip. There is no jarring jump or confusing passage of time between the two shots.

Bad example 1: A woman is drinking a cup of tea. The first shot shows the waiter walking over to her table with a teapot. The next shot shows her mid-sip as she's drinking her tea. The perceived time passing between shots makes the 'seam' between the two shots glaringly visible and jarring.

Good example 2: A shot of an interviewee cuts to a different angle during a pause. Hence, the dialogue continues without missed words from one shot to the next.

Bad example 2: A shot of an interviewee cuts to a different angle while talking, and half a word is cut off, resulting in an audible jump rather than a visual one.

Even if you seamlessly cut from one shot to another so that movement and dialogue match up, the jump will be noticeable if the color isn't the same in both shots. This is one of the reasons why shooting the same scene under the same lighting, at the same time of day, and generally under the same circumstances is crucial.

Tip 1: B-roll footage can be incredibly important for fixing shots that don't match up seamlessly. You can insert a piece of B-roll footage to disguise the jump.

Tip 2: Jumps can be fixed by cutting to a shot from a different angle or more close-up. It can't be just a little more close-up, though. It has to be a big difference; otherwise, you'll still notice a jump.

Tip 3: We told you to ditch the transition effects way back in Chapter One. If you edit your footage seamlessly, those transition effects won't be necessary to hide the jumps.

KEEP SCENES AND SHOTS SHORT

The concept of keeping shots short while shooting is also applicable during editing. You don't want to drag out a scene or a shot longer than is necessary for the audience to get the message you're trying to convey. Filling a scene with too much footage drags it out, and you risk your audience getting bored and switching off.

For example, imagine you're shooting a scene where two people arrange to meet at a cafe and then meet up. You don't need to film their entire conversation or a long cab ride to the cafe unless it's crucial to your story. You only need a short shot where all the audience hears of the conversation is that they're going to meet up and a short shot of the cab ride, which takes up no more than a few seconds.

DITCH THE "HAVE TO" SHOTS

You know the shots we're talking about. They're the ones you feel you "have to" include for some reason even though they're bad, unnecessary, or you just don't have time in your video duration. We're talking about the kinds of shots that make you say:

- "So-and-so will be offended/angry if I don't include them."
- "It was so hard to shoot. I don't want to leave it out."
- "I know it doesn't really help my video, but I love this shot."
- "If I don't include it, I wasted all that time and those resources for nothing."

TONE DOWN THE GRAPHIC DETAIL

Graphics could help or hurt your video, depending on when you use them. There's a time and place for graphics. If you're in doubt, leave it out. So, how do you know when and when not to use graphics?

When to use graphics:

- Video title graphics help identify the video. Make sure they're not too wordy.
- End credits do what they say. They give credit where credit is due. Don't give someone credit if they had nothing to do with the video.
- Entertaining graphics can work from time to time, like speech bubbles. Pop-up graphics need to deliver shock and drama or outright hilarious comedy for them to work.
- Identifying information can be useful to include a time, date, or place.

When you should steer clear of graphics:

- Don't tell your audience information they don't need to know. If the information isn't helpful or crucial, don't provide it.
- Don't use facts or figures you don't actually need, even if you think you do. It probably shouldn't be a video if you're trying to give viewers loads of facts or statistics throughout.

Graphics need to have a purpose. If they don't have an explicit reason for being there, ditch them. Unnecessary graphics make your video seem amateurish, or like you think your audience is not smart enough to get the visual message, and they distract from the visuals.

BREAKING THE NO TRANSITIONS RULE

There can be times and reasons for breaking some rules, and we did say to avoid transitions. However, transitions could be very useful in one particular situation:

You have two sequential shots you absolutely have to use, but there is a jarring jump at the cut between them. It's usually best to use a short B-roll clip to disguise the jump, but that's not always possible. In this case, you can opt to go overboard on the transition effect. Make it grand. Make it 'loud'. Make it enhance the jump. Sometimes highlighting a mistake is the best way to disguise it. It's like "hiding in plain sight".

VIDEO EDITING TIPS AND HACKS

Video editing can be daunting and even intimidating for beginners. So, getting all the help you can get goes a long way to make your life easier while learning the ropes. Here are some practical tips and hacks for your editing project.

The 321 rule: Always have three copies of the footage you will use for your video. Use two separate devices, such as hard drives, and store one of the devices off-site. This prevents data loss in case of corrupt files, damaged, lost, or corrupt devices, or damage to the building one of the devices is in.

Tutorials: As a beginner, watching tutorials and following along on a practice project of your own can be a useful way to learn techniques and video editing software.

Workflow efficiency: How you file your footage, images, graphics, audio, and so on can make your life easier or turn editing into a nightmare. Create an organized filing system to keep track of every file and part of your project.

BOTTOM LINE

Learning to edit a video is a process of trial and error. You're not going to be able to watch a couple of tutorials or read a few articles, and suddenly you're an editing pro. It's a skill that takes loads of practice to master. As you edit more videos, you'll notice your editing skills improving. Once you have an edited video, it's time to post that baby online, and that's what we'll be tackling in the next chapter.

17

SHARING YOUR VIDEO

"You're operating in a world where one good video can lead to a massive social following."

–Mike Henry

Once you've made your way through planning, filming, and editing your video, it's time to get it out there and get it seen. In this chapter, we will cover basic search optimization tips as well as advice for hosting your videos on various platforms.

PICK THE RIGHT PLATFORM

With various video-hosting platforms out there, picking the right one can seem impossible. Here's a rundown of the most popular video-hosting platforms and their pros and cons to help you decide.

You should ask yourself three questions before you even start comparing video-hosting platforms:

- Who is your audience, and which sites are they already using to view videos?
- How do you want your audience-content interaction to play out?
- What technical aspects of your content may become limitations (video duration, topic, file size, video quality, etc.)

Facebook

The pros:

- Content is moderated well
- Offers full optimization for mobile devices and hosting live video
- Hosting is free
- You can stream live
- It's geared toward social interaction
- It's the world's biggest social network
- There are no in-video adverts
- Videos hosted on the platform itself have a higher likelihood of being seen than video links shared from other platforms

The cons:

- Searching for older videos hosted on Facebook itself becomes harder
- The analytics aren't great
- Videos are subject to technical limitations, such as size, frames per second, and resolution
- Videos have a short visibility span, moving down newsfeeds pretty quickly

YouTube

The pros:

- It's totally free
- Once verified, you aren't subject to storage or upload limitations
- The analytics are great
- Videos aren't subject to technical limitations
- You can create different channels for different products of brands
- You can stream live
- It has a gobsmackingly massive audience
- YouTube is owned by Google, providing powerful SEO and making YouTube-hosted videos rank at the top of searches
- Offers full optimization for mobile devices and hosting live video

The cons:

- YouTube videos don't normally enjoy as many comments or shares compared to Facebook-hosted videos
- Moderation of comments isn't great, and they can make your message less impactful
- The content of your competitors or even ads for their content can be shown near your videos
- YouTube's in-video ads are a turn-off for viewers

Instagram

The pros:

- Facebook owns Instagram, making sharing and comments more powerful
- Completely mobile
- It's good for business-to-customer (B2C) interaction
- It's popular with younger audiences
- The editing tools help if you're on a tight budget
- You can unleash your creativity with in-app filters and features

The cons:

- Designed for mobile, and use on a desktop is limited
- Photos are Instagram's main focus

TikTok

The pros:

- Brand-to-influencer collaboration is a cinch
- It's aimed at mobile and is one of the most popular devices to view video for younger generations
- It's available in various countries and languages, offering exposure to new markets
- The newer generations are the target audience
- You can get creative while raising brand awareness
- You get exposure to a wide audience

The cons:

- Advertising is expensive
- Influencers are favored above paid advertised content; popularity is key
- Older viewers aren't likely to use TikTok
- Text and image posts are limited
- You need to consistently create viral content
- Businesses need to be more careful because of the usually comical and sensationalist content posted on TikTok

Vimeo

The pros:

- Analytics are good

- Videos rank on the platform because they are well made and have quality content and not just because they are popular (some platforms have a heavy bias toward popularity even if the video isn't that great)
- It's the video hosting platform of choice for creatives
- The community is more supportive, with fewer internet trolls
- There are no in-video adverts
- Videos are not subject to technical limitations
- You can customize the video player with brand-related colors, logos, thumbnails, and features

The cons:

- Businesses don't get free accounts
- Different price plans have some technical limitations
- Google shows favoritism toward YouTube over Vimeo in web searches, resulting in less visibility
- Smaller audiences than other platforms

BASIC SEARCH OPTIMIZATION TIPS

Search engine optimization is a large part of how videos get seen. If the search engines don't index your video, nobody will find it. However, SEO is a vast subject that could easily fill an entire book by itself. Here are some handy tips for getting the basics of optimization right:

- Pick the right platform: Posting to the wrong platform can hurt your video exposure. Pick the right platform by comparing your video objectives with the pros and cons of each platform.
- Avoid relying only on organic SEO principles to get your video seen. SEO is ever-changing and imperfect. Paid ads can often help increase reach and viewership.
- Choose keywords carefully based on audience profiles and market research but avoid keyword stuffing, overusing, or using too many different keywords.
- Create an exciting and engaging title and description using keywords to get your video found and entice viewers.
- Select an appropriate category that your video falls under.
- Update video descriptions to get platforms to re-assess your video and rank it higher as an updated video.
- Use an engaging thumbnail to entice viewers to watch your video but avoid clickbait, which will annoy and alienate viewers.
- Use hashtags to help drive traffic to your video.
- Use keywords in your video file name.

UPLEVELING VIDEOS
EVERYWHERE

If you've gone back to your early videos and compared them to what you're producing now that you're working on your skills and implementing the techniques you've learned here, you've probably already noticed the incredible difference… and now you have a chance to help someone else experience that same growth.

Simply by leaving your honest opinion of this book on Amazon, you'll show new readers where they can find all the information they need to improve their video content.

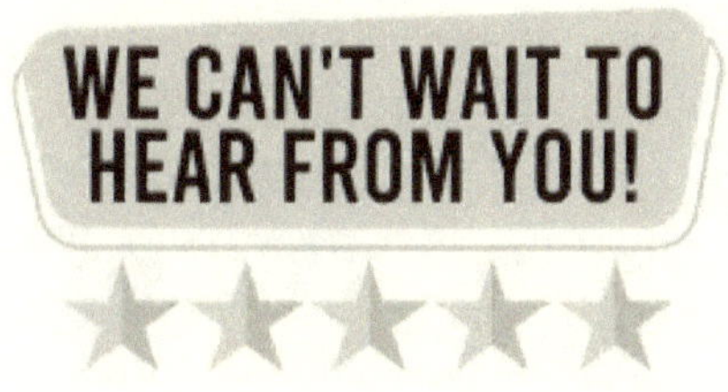

We can't thank you enough for your support… and we can't wait to see the results as video makers everywhere grow in confidence and quality.

Please visit the link below or scan the QR code to leave feedback on Amazon.

https://www.amazon.com/review/create-review/?asin=1739816285

CONCLUSION

Anyone can press record on their mobile phone and shoot a little video. That may suffice for sharing with family and friends. It's not going to cut it for a wider audience, especially if you want people to click that 'like' button or monetize them. Making a video look like an amateur hasn't shot takes time, know-how, and skill. As they say, anything worth having is worth working for; good video-making skills are one of those things. The good news is that we've covered the basic steps and principles of what you need to know as a beginner video maker to start making videos that look more professional.

We've discussed a wide range of topics that are vital to understand, such as:

- the equipment you do need and what isn't strictly necessary

- dividing up your video budget so you're spending enough money where it matters and not wasting it where it doesn't
- planning your video so you have the right kinds of goals and can effectively write a story and script
- a variety of filming techniques that will help you improve your videos, starting today
- different lighting techniques to help you properly showcase your subject and create the appropriate mood
- the computer hardware and software requirements for editing a video to polish off what you already filmed using the techniques we've taught you
- how to edit your video so it looks more professional
- discussing popular video-hosting platforms and their pros and cons to help you decide which one is the best fit for your video
- and we've covered a host of tips and tricks to make learning to produce better quality videos so much easier

You've come to know that learning to make a more professional-looking video doesn't come easy, but you're not deterred. Why? We've armed you with everything you need to easily and quickly learn the ropes. You now have the knowledge to take your videos to the next level and stop making lousy videos.

Just remember, even if your videos don't look like a professional production team, put them together right away; they will improve with time. It takes trial, error, and practice to master the principles we've covered. However, you're committed to making better videos, and as long as you set the right SMART goals and have the patience to master these exceptional skills, you'll keep getting better. You'll develop a video maker's eye and learn to intuit shots and improvisations. Soon, you won't even have to think about lighting, positioning, scene elements, and various other aspects of video-making. They will start to come to you naturally!

Take some time to implement these techniques and principles for a while. Then go back and look at the videos you shot and produced in the very beginning. You'll probably be surprised at how much you've improved and how far you've come. Keep filming and practicing, and we guarantee you'll keep getting better.

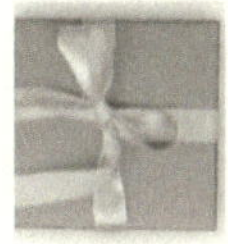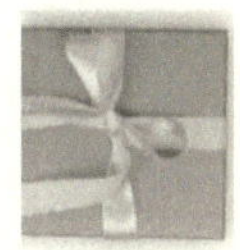

A Free Bonus To Our Readers

To get you started on using videos for social media, we have created:

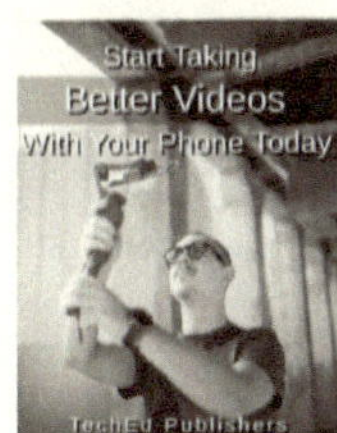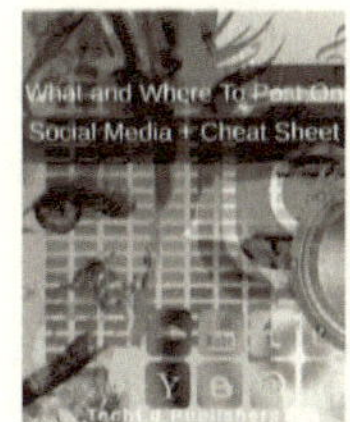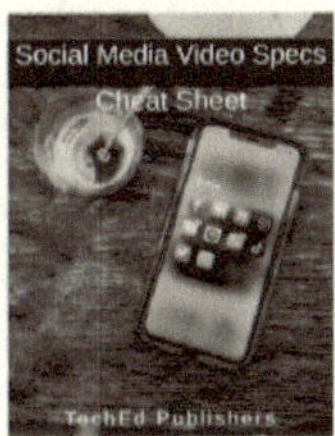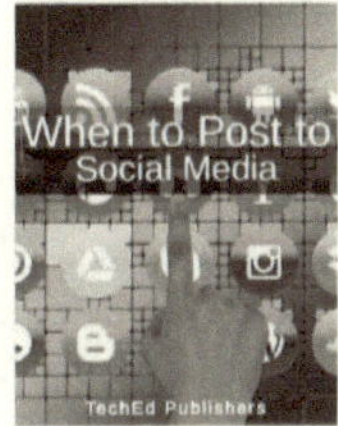

Free Bonus #1

Start Taking Better Videos with Your Phone Today

Free Bonus #2

What and Where to Post on Social Media + Cheat Sheet

Free Bonus #3

Social Media Video Specs Cheat Sheet

Free Bonus #4

When to Post to Social Media

With these free bonuses, you will

- Unlock the secrets to taking stunning videos with your phone today!

- Get a handy cheat sheet to guide you in creating the perfect content for each social media platform!

- Get a guide to create videos using the specifications of your chosen platform

- Determine the ideal times to post on various social media platforms and maximize the impact of your posts!

To get your free bonuses, please visit the link or scan the QR code below and let us know the email address to send it to.

pages.techedpublishers.com/bonus/vmfb

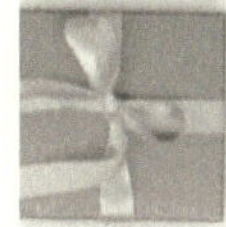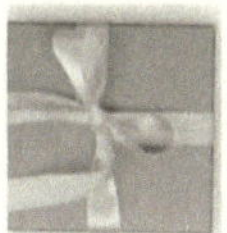

REFERENCES

"3 point lighting.svg" by Theonlysiletnbob, Wikimedia Commons is in the Public Domain, CC0

73 of the best quotes about filmmaking — FILM CRUX. (2019, January 7). FILM CRUX. https://www.filmcrux.com/blog/best-filmmaking-quotes

"Headroom (photographic framing)" by Wikipedia is licensed under CC BY-SA 4.0

10 tips for shooting video outside. (2020, March 3). BombBomb. https://bombbomb.com/blog/shooting-video-outside-outdoors-sun-lighting-tips/

180-degree rule. (2022, November 1). In Wikipedia. https://en.wikipedia.org/wiki/180-degree_rule

180 degree rule. (2019, May 8). Opening Class. https://openingclass.com/2019/05/08/180-degree-rule/

Aldredge, J. (2021, June 21). To break or not to break: The significance of the 180-degree rule. Premium Beat. https://www.premiumbeat.com/blog/180-degree-rule-cinematography/

Baker, L. (2020, July 3). Back to basics: The rule of thirds in filmmaking. Premium Beat. https://www.premiumbeat.com/blog/rule-of-thirds-filmmaking/

Bennett, R. (2022, January 14). Indoor natural lighting tips. Filmora Wondershare. https://filmora.wondershare.com/vlogger/how-to-get-natural-lighting-to-shoot-videos-indoors.html

Bernazzani, S. (2013). How to write a video script (Template + video). Hubspot. https://blog.hubspot.com/marketing/how-to-write-a-video-script-ht

Berry, S. (2021, March 1). Every type of light modifier for video you need to know. Videomaker. https://www.videomaker.com/how-to/lighting/every-type-of-light-modifier-for-video-you-need-to-know/

Betts, M. (n.d.). Three ways to break the rule of thirds by Mike Betts, Photocrowd co-founder. Photocrowd. https://www.photocrowd.com/blog/10-three-ways-break-rule-thirds/

Chamoiseau, C. (2020, April 1). PC specs for video editing: A comprehensive guide. Improve Video Studio. https://improvevideostudio.com/pc-specs-for-video-editing-a-comprehensive-guide/

Currier, A. (2018, June 8). The Wistia guide to video metrics. Wistia. https://wistia.com/learn/marketing/guide-to-video-metrics

Deguzman, K. (2020, July 20). What is key light? Definition and examples in photography and film. Studio Binder. https://www.studiobinder.com/blog/what-is-key-light-definition/

Deguzman, K. (2021, January 24). What is practical lighting in film? Tips and techniques explained. Studio Binder. https://www.studiobinder.com/blog/what-is-practical-lighting-in-film/

Dempsey, J. (2021, October 5). Rule of thirds in video: The essential guide. Digital Photography School. https://digital-photography-school.com/rule-of-thirds-in-video/

Ebiner, P. (2016, September 26). Choosing a background for your videos. Videoschool. https://www.videoschool.com/choosing-background-videos/

Ebiner, P. (2018, December 18). Using natural light for video production. Videoschool. https://www.videoschool.com/using-natural-light-for-video-production/

Ebiner, P. (2018, October 16). How to choose the right camera for video production. Videoschool. https://www.videoschool.com/how-to-choose-the-right-camera-for-video-production/

Gold, N. (2019, March 1). Video lightning guide part 1: Different types of light. Film Daft. https://filmdaft.com/video-lighting-guide-part-1-different-types-of-light/

Gold, N. (2019, March 18). Video lighting guide part 3: Basic lighting setups. Film Daft. https://filmdaft.com/video-lighting-guide-part-3-basic-lighting-setups/

Gold, N. (2019, March 5). Video lighting guide part 2: Lamps and modifications. Film Daft. https://filmdaft.com/video-lighting-guide-part-2-lamps-and-modifications/

Gula, D. (2020, March 4). 4 types of microphones for filmmaking and vlogging. (2020 edition). Sound Stripe. https://www.soundstripe.com/blogs/4-types-of-microphones-for-filmmaking-and-vlogging

Hellerman, J. (2019, May 7). Types of film lights (and how to use them). No Film School. https://nofilmschool.com/types-of-film-lights

How to choose a backdrop for your video. (2017, December 1). True Film

Production. https://truefilmproduction.com/choose-backdrop-video/

How to choose a microphone for your videos. (2017, March 30). Razor Social. https://www.razorsocial.com/choose-microphone-for-your-videos/

How to choose video editing software. (2016, November 2). The DIY Video Editor. https://diyvideoeditor.com/choose-video-editing-software/

Huffaker, A. (2021, October 27). Why audio is so important to your video. Storyboard Media Company. https://storyboardmedia.co/insights/why-audio-is-so-important-to-your-video/

Hyman, I. (2019, April 22). How to turn a hard light into a soft light: An important video lighting technique. Izzy Video. https://www.izzyvideo.com/hard-light-soft-light/

Kahn, J. (2021). Reasons to use a camcorder instead of DSLR/mirrorless cameras in field production. B & H Photo & Electronics Corporation. https://www.bhphotovideo.com/explora/video/tips-and-solutions/reasons-to-use-a-camcorder-instead-of-dslrmirrorless-cameras-in-field

Knott, R. (2020, April 7). Why people stop watching your videos (and how to avoid it!). Tech Smith. https://www.techsmith.com/blog/why-people-stop-watching-videos/

Kosmala, D. (2021, April 1). Video production equipment: Level up your content with these 12 tools. Uscreen. https://www.uscreen.tv/blog/video-production-equipment/

Kroll, N. (2013, October 7). How to shoot with natural light: 10 tips. Indie Wire. https://www.indiewire.com/2013/10/how-to-shoot-with-natural-light-10-tips-34217/

Kroll, N. (2015). 3 basic tips for creating soft light. Premium Beat. https://www.premiumbeat.com/blog/3-basic-tips-creating-soft-light/

Lannom, S. (2020, March 9). Three-point video lighting: Key, fill, & backlight setup guide. Studio Binder. https://www.studiobinder.com/blog/three-point-lighting-setup/

Lebendig, U. (2021, April 9). Hard light vs soft light. (Differences & how to create them). Shotkit. https://shotkit.com/hard-light-vs-soft-light/

Levigne, C. (2020, may 20). Choosing a background for your video. Wistia. https://wistia.com/learn/production/choosing-a-background

Maher, M. (2015, October 21). How to choose the best camera for your video production. Shutterstock. https://www.shutterstock.com/blog/how-to-choose-the-best-video-camera-for-production/

Master Class Staff. (2020, November 8). How to set up video lighting: 4 tips for lighting video. Master Class. https://www.masterclass.com/articles/how-to-set-up-video-lighting#how-to-set-up-lighting-for-video

Master Class Staff. (2021, August 23). Film 101: Understanding film lighting. Master Class. https://www.masterclass.com/articles/film-101-understanding-film-lighting

McCoy, E. (2020, September 24). How to develop a video content strategy. Killer Visual Strategies. https://killervisualstrategies.com/blog/how-to-develop-a-video-content-strategy.html

McGregor, L. (2022, January 31). How to shoot interior locations with limited lighting. Premium Beat. https://www.premiumbeat.com/blog/shoot-interior-locations-limited-lighting/

McIntire, J. (2016, June 5). Natural light versus artificial light: Which is better? Digital Photography School. https://digital-photography-school.com/natural-light-versus-artificial-light-which-is-better/

Mister, M. (2019, August 30). What specs do I need for video editing? Pro Max Media Technology Solutions. https://www.promax.com/blog/what-specs-do-i-need-for-video-editing

Morrison, A. (2019, December 17). Setting smart goals for your video content. Beverly Boy Productions. https://beverlyboy.com/corporate-marketing-video-production/setting-smart-goals-for-your-video-content/

Newberry, C. (2020, July 8). How to find and target your social media audience (Free template), Hootsuite Inc. https://blog.hootsuite.com/target-market/

Powell, L. (2020, January 9). 5 ways to identify the right target audience for your brand. CMA Solutions. https://cmasolutions.com/blog/5-ways-to-identify-the-right-target-audience-for-your-brand/

Ramsay, C. (2016, July 6). Choosing the right video platform for your content. Dragonlight Films. https://dragonlightfilms.com/blog/choosing-the-right-video-platform-for-your-content

Ruiz Ricard, J. (2018, December 6). 20 types of shots, camera angles, and movements all videographers should know. Wix Photography. https://www.wix.com/blog/photography/2018/12/06/types-of-shots/

San Filippo, C. (2019, September 20). Filming 101: Types of camera shots and angles. Polarpro. https://www.polarprofilters.com/blogs/polarpro/filmmaking-101-types-of-camera-shots-and-angles

Sarika. (2021, December 20). YouTube equipment: The only guide you will ever need to create YouTube videos. inVideo. https://invideo.io/blog/youtube-equipment/

Schenker, M. (2015, September 10). So what's really better: Artificial or natural light? Contrastly. https://contrastly.com/artificial-or-natural-light/

Sherman, A. (n.d.). What is a storyboard? Storyboard That. https://www.storyboardthat.com/articles/e/what-is-a-storyboard

Stancheva, T. (2022, February 24). 24 noteworthy video consumption statistics (2022 edition). Tech Jury. https://techjury.net/blog/video-consumption-statistics/

Sudhakaran, S. (2019, February 25). 15 essential camera shots, angles and movements. Wolfcrow. https://wolfcrow.com/15-essential-camera-shots-angles-and-movements/

The Boomer Consumer. (2021, February 11). Camcorders vs. DSLRs 2021 edition. YouTube. https://www.youtube.com/watch?v=u_3nc1WZqLs

Theonlysilentbob. (2008, February 21). 3 point lighting.svg. Wiki Commons. https://commons.wikimedia.org/wiki/File:3_point_lighting.svg

Tips for shooting video in natural light. (2019, June 13). Canon Australia. https://www.canon.com.au/explore/tips-for-shooting-video-in-natural-light

Twigg, M. (2020, November 17). How to write a video script that will keep people watching. Play Play. https://playplay.com/blog/how-to-write-a-video-script/

Video composition rules: Establishing, medium & close-up shots from Nikon. (2013, December 16). Nikon USA. https://www.nikonusa.com/en/learn-and-explore/a/tips-and-techniques/video-composition-rules-establishing-medium-and-close-up-shots.html

Weitz, A. (2021). A guide to filters and lenses. B & H Photo & Electronics Corporation. https://www.bhphotovideo.com/explora/photography/buying-guide/a-guide-to-filters-for-lenses

Wind noise Reduction: How to remove wind noise from video. (2020, December 5). Akaso. https://www.akasotech.com/blogs/remove-wind-noise-from-video

Zeke. (2016, October 8). 10 cinematography tricks for working with only natural light. New York Film Academy. https://www.nyfa.edu/student-resources/10-cinematography-tricks-for-working-with-only-natural-lighting/

www.ingramcontent.com/pod-product-compliance
Lightning Source LLC
Chambersburg PA
CBHW021828090726
47818CB00077BA/87